America
is John the Baptist of Nations

The Last Nation
To Be Created by Jesus

KENNETH D. JONGELING

WESTBOW
P R E S S®
A DIVISION OF THOMAS NELSON
& ZONDERVAN

WestBow Press books may be ordered through booksellers or by contacting:

WestBow Press
A Division of Thomas Nelson & Zondervan
1663 Liberty Drive
Bloomington, IN 47403
www.westbowpress.com
844-714-3454

Scripture quotations marked (NLT) are taken from the Holy Bible, New Living Translation, copyright ©1996, 2004, 2015 by Tyndale House Foundation. Used by permission of Tyndale House Publishers, a Division of Tyndale House Ministries, Carol Stream, Illinois 60188. All rights reserved.

ISBN: 978-1-6642-7159-3 (sc)
ISBN: 978-1-6642-7161-6 (hc)
ISBN: 978-1-6642-7160-9 (e)

Library of Congress Control Number: 2022912337

Print information available on the last page.

WestBow Press rev. date: 09/27/2022

Contents

Introduction

If someone were to say that I love my country more than Jesus, I would answer, "How could I do such a thing? I know that Jesus loved me first, but my country does not even know me, unless I owe it taxes."

God made me part of one of the biggest gifts in the history of His creation—Christ was the best—and I owe Him thanks, gratitude, glory, and honor. The purpose of this writing is not to express discouragement or to look into specific actions that might take place in the future. I believe that God is preparing me for the harsh and evil things that are very near. It is my intent to help prepare my fellow American citizens so that my Christian brothers and sisters will do what Christ advised: to keep their lamps filled with oil.

We will consider scripture, history, some ethics, and some politics. All these factors would be in any description of society, and there would be prejudices involved with any understanding of events. There are, however, two terms used in the area of politics that I find offensive: *liberal* and *conservative*. I might appear to be a conservative—at least, I might seem too conservative to some very important people in my life—but I'm not someone who is making the news. I find that the terms *liberal* and *conservative* are too broad to describe the two groups, but to describe the mindset of individuals, I must use these words.

As I was writing this book, my mind kept telling me there was something that I needed to say before finishing this work. My intent in writing this book was to share my thoughts on why this nation was created. I believe it was created to be an example to the world so that other nations could have a chance to be more just and to allow their citizens to have the freedoms we enjoy. Some have come close but haven't been able to achieve the spirit with which the United States was created.

I hope this book will give readers the opportunity to prepare for the future. Scripture records Christ's story of the servants who were waiting for the bridegroom. Half of them used their waiting time by getting additional oil for their lamps, while the other half slept. When the bridegroom finally arrived, those who had the wisdom to get more oil were the ones allowed into the wedding festivities because the others were gone, getting new oil. This message is for the believers, for those who are prepared for what I believe will be a very troublesome future.

For those who do not acknowledge what scripture describes as a troublesome future, the Antichrist will convince leaders to guide their supporters to adhere to and accept dangerous life-changing policies. They can continue to mock and ridicule our beliefs; that is up to them.

I will not offer the message that we often read from other authors. The inspiration we receive from individuals such as Phil Robertson, author of *The Theft of America's Soul*; businessman Mike Lindell; and Rev. Norman Vincent Peale, author of *The Power of Positive Thinking*, is meaningful, enlightening, and uplifting, and it gives us the needed desire to change our lives or our current goals. My purpose here is to offer reasons why we should consider what might be in the near future. The expectation of the return of Christ has been in the minds and hearts of Christians for nearly two thousand years. Even Jesus's disciples hoped to see His return, so this is not something new.

I believe, however, that we must consider an updated version of this matter. With each day that passes, we get older and closer to death; with each passing day, we also get closer to Christ's return. We must consider, however, historical factors, which I believe will bring us closer to understanding that which no previous generation could describe as signs of how close we are to the end of history.

Why do I have such strong feelings for this nation? My reasons relate to the following:

1. I experienced the death of my sister.
2. A couple of years after my sister's death, our pastor preached a series of sermons.
3. Following those sermons, I received a message from Christ.
4. Years later, Rev. Dr. Virgil Rogers told his Old Testament history class about God's creation of nations that represented God in history.
5. I eventually expanded on his theory.
6. These events brought me to the conclusion that the United States is the John the Baptist of nations.

This book is based on two principles. The first is from Matthew 21:43, which tells us: "What I mean is that the Kingdom of God will be taken away from you and given to a nation that will produce the proper fruit." The second principle relates to the definition of *prophecy* from *The Interpreter's Dictionary of the Bible*: "For prophetism may legitimately be defined as the understanding of history which accepts meaning only in terms of divine concern, divine purpose, divine participation."

Thus, as we consider the events of history, whether in regard to personal history or world history, we need to look at how we perceive those events—are they a concern to God? Also, how do the events reflect God's purpose? These elements are intertwined, making it difficult to distinguish between concern and purpose, but if we recognize God's participation in our events, the concern and purpose become clearer. We must evaluate historical events from these perspectives before we can understand the role of nations in the kingdom of grace, created by Jesus Christ.

I've offered examples of what I mean with regard to God's concern and purpose and how He participated. In the story of Israel's development, people became distrustful of the governing arrangement under which they were living; that was the time of the judges. They came to Samuel and asked that he establish a king, as in all the other nations. After seeking advice from God, Samuel was advised to give them a king. Samuel then told his people:

> This is how a king will treat you. The king will draft your sons into his army and make them run before his chariots ... The king will take your daughters from you and force them to cook and bake and make perfumes for him ... He will take a tenth of your harvest and distribute it among his officers and attendants ... When the day comes, you will beg for relief from this king you are demanding, but the Lord will not help you. (1 Samuel 8:11–19)

In Jeremiah, we learn that Jeremiah, who was a prophet (a spokesman for God), told the people to stay in Jerusalem and not to be afraid of the king of Babylon. He said that if they did go to Egypt, God would bring terrible things upon them. Still, their reply was:

> You Lie! The Lord our God hasn't forbidden us to go to Egypt! Baruch son of Neriah has convince you to say this, so we will stay here and be killed by the Babylonians or be carried into exile. (Jeremiah 43: 2–3)

These two illustrations demonstrate the people's concerns, but they also reflect God's concerns and His participation. These illustrations represent conservative political ideas; that is, God has concerns, and He participates in history, which differs from the general opinions of the liberals, who might argue that the people had a right to choose the form of government they wanted and that they had the right to go where they wanted. I, however, accept them (the people's concerns and that God has concerns) as truths, regardless of the political opinion that someone might interpret them to be.

Some might argue that the sky, on a beautiful, cloudless day, is not blue but green. They have the right to believe that is true, but that does not mean the sky, if it *is* green, is God's concern or that He participated.

Chapter 1

W hy do I have such strong feelings for the United States of America? These feelings began when I was twelve years old, with the death of my sister. It was then I began trying to understand God's concerns, purpose, and participation with regard to my sister's life and death. As I saw it, God's intent was not so much to create the usual sibling rivalry and growing pains as it was to build a platform by which His glory would be brought into light.

I'll admit that I have failed to carry forward many of the things I learned from my relationship with my sister, but there was a learning process. Some events surrounding her death, however, have had lasting effects. One of these is my memory of my father, falling to his knees with tears streaming down his cheeks. Here was a giant of a man, someone I had never seen cry, pulling me tight and sobbing, "She dead! Bonnie is dead!" That scene has entered my mind many times.

I heard a story of a proclaimed atheist who acted in a way that, for me, described a significant difference between good and evil. He and his wife decided to kill themselves in their living room, resulting in their thirteen-year-old daughter finding them when she came home from school.

The first scene shows the pronounced love of a father, on his knees with uncontrolled tears, the second shows a father who left his daughter with the everlasting memory of finding the bodies of her parents and wondering why.

Another memory from those moments was when I managed to get out of Dad's tight hold, and I went to Mom, who was crying. As I hugged her, I asked why Bonnie had died. I'll never forget her response to my twelve-year-old self: a tiny blood vessel had burst in my sister's brain, and her head had filled with blood. Mom said that the doctor had told her that even if Bonnie had been in the emergency room when the blood vessel burst, there still would not have been anything the doctors could have done.

That was true in 1958, but medical science has truly advanced because today, if similar situations are caught early enough, lives can be saved.

The importance at that moment, however, was that I suddenly realized how vulnerable human life is and how much we need to depend upon God.

Accepting these truths as expressions of God's concern for us has benefited my understanding of life and has allowed me to put into perspective many things that have happened; I understand that God knows what we can deal with in life.

During my sister's funeral, God revealed to me an after-life experience. This was a vivid scene of my sister, standing next to Jesus. I could feel a joy and peace that I thought no one could ever experience in this world—of course, we can feel the joy and peace of heaven, but those moments are short and must be recognized as such.

I also experienced a feeling of power that held me captive long after the revelation had ended. For years, I believed it was simply power—a power that God possesses that allows Him to do anything He desires. I felt this power as the world sees it. For example, the world sees a tornado as an act of nature, the power of nature. The world sees the power that Donald J. Trump used to build the border wall as merely the power of the presidency, which was used to reinforce the power and status of the Trump empire. But as I now understand the power of God and His concern for the nation He created, the building of the wall was to protect God's people, the American citizens. Another power that then-president Trump used was social media. People saw Trump's purpose, in texting the American people, as his method to build his prestige and maintain his authoritarian position. I believe, however, that this power in using social media was granted by God to show us our choices and help us decide which way we wanted our nation to proceed.

Do we want to follow the historical principles of our founding fathers, who thoroughly debated the differences between a democratic republic and a totalitarian form of government (socialism, communist socialism, or dictatorship)? Through the use of social media, Trump made clear to the American people what was happening. He could tell us, but he could not force us to believe. He explained that we had lost so any of our rights because of unelected government employees creating laws and regulations.

We must consider one more factor with regard to the issue of power, something I classify as a negative effect. I never have considered myself as a lazy person. I've never been afraid of work, and only once, for a few months, did my wife and I depend on government aid. However, the power I witnessed while with my sister and Jesus seemed to make me rely on God's power to get things done. So rather than forging ahead and do the work I thought I needed to be done so that God could then do what he wanted done, I would pause to see what God would do before I acted. Eventually, I realized that the power of God was His love, which allowed Him to finish the things that we do. It is then that the concern and purpose that makes us and molds us shows the participation of God at work within us.

It was this recognition that formed my profound interest in how God works in our world. I no longer wanted to sit in the back pew; instead, I listened intensely to sermons, Sunday school teachers, and youth group leaders—both adults and fellow students. I also began listening to my secular school teachers and the readings they required.

I've often joked that when God was creating me, and He said, "Give him a brain," I thought He said *rain*, so I covered my head. As a result, most of the things I've learned have not remained with me.

But time moves on, and so must we. Fast-forward a couple of years to when our pastor, Reverend Ralph Cortis, started a series of messages, beginning with Genesis 1:1. He showed how each historical story told of God's love and the eventual life and sacrifice of Jesus. When he got to the creation of God's first nation, Reverend Cortis spoke of something that very few ministers are willing to preach.

Because of social and political correctness, we have been told not to make our nation seem superior to other nations, and so we are not allowed to compare our history with the biblical accounts of the creation of Israel. It was this comparison, however, that made me see the work that God is doing in the world today.

Let's consider a couple of examples, the first being the importance of the chosen people being held as slaves. The first pilgrims (or any of the many other people who came to the New World) were not slaves, but they were held in bondage to the state church in their homelands, where they were prohibited from freely expressing themselves or living their lives in the way they felt God wanted them to live. They decided to escape to the New World, where they could create new communities, based on their own understanding of God's grace, free from the national church and regulations of the state.

The second similarity between the creation of Israel and the

United States was the body of water that the people needed to cross. For the Israelites, there was the miracle of the separation of the Red Sea so that they could walk across on foot. The pilgrims of the seventeenth century, however, had to rely on boats, which, in my opinion, was suicidal. Consider the words the people read in their scripture:

> The mighty oceans have roared, O Lord, the mighty oceans roar like thunder, the mighty oceans roar as they pound the shore, But mightier than the violent raging of the seas, mightier than the breakers on the shore-the Lord above is mightier than these! (Psalms 93:3–4)

Yet they climbed aboard and sailed across the mighty Atlantic in wooden ships. They did not have cruise ships with luxury accommodations, lounges with live bands, and swimming pools and fancy restaurants. They experienced rainstorms and strong winds that blew waves into the boats, but like the Israelites, they did not have to swim across.

Another similarity is that in both cases, the people spent time in the wilderness. The Israelites' experience took place in a barren open area, where food and water basically did not exist. Their survival was completely dependent upon God's providing food (manna from heaven) and water (from rocks). The pilgrims, however, had green vegetation, trees for cover and warmth, and wild game they could hunt for food. Neither group moved into condos or apartments with swimming pools and recreational facilities.

Both parties started their nations with independent communities. The Israelites, after entering the territory that God had promised them, organized small communities that were guided and protected by judges. Judges were men who settled disagreements and generally acted as mayors. The people depended on God as their leader, but they looked to the judges as God's representatives. Our first settlers also started with small communities. They, too, looked to God as their leader and supporter, but they relied on the reading of scripture and their writing of laws, and they depended on elected men to be their leaders. In both instances, the people rejected the idea of having a king and looked to God as their King.

Still another example of the similarity of the two nations includes clearing the land, which, unfortunately, involved dealing with those who already were living in the territory. Organizing a united nation involved creating new forms of government, which included making many mistakes. In the creation of the New World, many mistakes were made by the new invaders, as well as the natives. The years of war and loss of lives on both sides reflect, in my opinion, the sinful nature of man, but that does not excuse the acts by individuals. Along with the physical hardships, there were many arguments and internal battles. The result was the Revolutionary War and the writing of our Constitution and the Bill of Rights. We have not yet written the closing acts for our nation, but God did create a nation that has been looked at with envy by other nations, who often have the desire to join our way of life.

We will see more similarities as we progress, but Reverend Cortis did stress one point: that Israel and the United States are different from other nations. This is something we must understand with regard to God's creation of a nation, compared to what man creates. When people act in accordance with God's creative power, they realize that God requires certain rules they need to follow. Those rules are given by the prophets God sent. Individuals warn us today, but they are expressing ideas already given to us in scripture.

I'll never forget the day at New Brunswick Theological Seminary when Dr. Koops and I met to discuss the work I'd need to do for my summer course in ethics. He told me that although the seminary was created to prepare individuals to be ministers and teachers for the church of Christ, I must answer one question: why would a seminary like this require its students to take a secular course in ethics? To put it another way, what right did the church have to bring the secular science of ethics into its teachings? Or what right did the church have to bring Christ into the secular science of ethics? Dr. Koops then told me to study the introduction and progress of existentialism, nationalism, and situational ethics from the beginning of the twentieth century to the middle of the 1950s.

The principal ideas of those philosophical expressions of life begin with the idea that men and women must create goals for themselves and for their nation. Once we have defined those goals, the principles of these philosophies state that we must do whatever is needed to make our goals a reality. If we must cheat to achieve our goals, that's what we must do. If we have to lie, so be it. If we must steal from our neighbor or from other countries, our goal is more important than what others might think or whatever they are living with. Making our goals a reality also might require that we kill, or, in the case of the nation, we may have to imprison or exile anyone who doesn't agree with us. We may even have to censor or take away the freedom that God has given us. All these acts may be accomplished by using situational ethics, which means we can take any event and twist or distort facts or actual words or show only the parts of the videos that highlight our purpose.

Those philosophical principles were used by Hitler and members of his political party, but the principles also are used today. Companies use them when they advertise the great advantage to shopping at their stores and for their products, while threatening or bullying employees and competitors or even blacklisting customers who express ideas that are counter to the philosophy of the corporation.

Chapter 2

I was in my sophomore English class when I heard a voice say, *What she is saying is true.*

"She" was the teacher, who was talking about the author of the book we were assigned to read and the history of the book's text.

The voice continued: *But what I have been telling you is also true.*

The voice was referring to the fact that as I read the book, I'd thought it was a modern-day book of Jeremiah, Isaiah, and Hosea—a book that explained why the United States would be destroyed.

The voice then said, *And before you die, you will see the destruction of your beloved nation.*

This was like a bolt of lightning, but surprisingly, I came back with the question: *Does that mean I will witness Your return?*

I then heard a chuckle, and it sounded like He was walking way as He said, *You know I do not know the date of My return, for God is the only one who knows that date.*

Of course, this all took place in my head, but it was so real that I was surprised I didn't get called on for an explanation. Just like the experience concerning the revelation about my sister, this was not sought after, which means it wasn't a hallucination. If I understand hallucinations correctly, they are thoughts or images that are sought after by using various methods, such as scented candles or various objects that are used to influence the minds of those seeking inspiration.

After many years of running—much like Jonah, which resulted in his being swallowed by a large fish and then spit out onto land—I attended a class on Old Testament history at New Brunswick Theological Seminary. Dr. Vigil Rogers observed that once God created his first nation, He has had a nation that represents Him since the fall of Israel. But with each new nation, there was a movement west. When the colonists believed their community was becoming too secular, they moved west, creating new communities (utopias). The result is that, today, Christians have no west to move to. As Christians, we must find ways to exist, or we will perish.

Let's consider the fact that Christians no longer have new, undeveloped territories to which we can move to escape the unforgiving, dividing nature and the continual degrading accusations of what Christians believe and cherish as principles to live our lives. Of course, these principles have always been mocked and scorned, and those who do so, although they think they are clever and enlightened, are actually rehashing Satan's evil philosophies. These expressions create problems today, as others have done throughout history, but although our forefathers could escape such vulgar actions by moving west, we don't have that option.

Let's also consider an additional point in this observation: that the Jewish nation was destroyed in AD 70, primarily because God had given them thirty-five years to accept Jesus Christ, but they rejected Him. "Christian" nations had one common fault: they truly disliked the Jews (because they blamed the Jews for killing their Savior). Then, in the early sixteenth century, the Christian Church and Western society had a major development known as the Reformation. As a result, for the first time in Christian history, the practice developed of studying and incorporating Old Testament teachings with the New Testament so that the common people could learn about the foundation of Christianity.

We are living in a Judeo-Christian society, and the importance of this religious and social advancement in the history of humankind is the finality of what God has for us. I believe that with the advancement of each of God's nations in history, humankind has been given improved standards of living, increased understanding of the purpose of why we were created, and the ability to form a more perfect union. Yet these improvements that God has offered us are the very things that the Left is trying to destroy. Their ideas are the same ideas that others have tried and have failed. They argue that previous attempts failed because they were not allowed to complete their objectives. Their objectives, however, were not allowed to be completed because they were created on false premises.

Every attempt to create a society based on equality and sharing of the wealth has resulted in the leaders of those attempts having the wealth and power they were rebelling against. Of course, that was what they sought from the beginning. US Representative Alexandria Ocasio-Cortez and her willing followers, including President Biden, all preach equality, yet their personal wealth has increased beyond everything any person needs for personal existence. They cling to that which they tell us is their objective to give to us, but their standard of living improves beyond any measure than we are given. In the process of their success, we have been forced to give up our right to achieve what we seek. Our freedom to gather as small groups is being taken from us so that we cannot share what we have with others. These things are destroying the Judeo-Christian society that so many from around the world have sought to join.

We must consider other signs that show how close we are to the end of history. One of those signs is the advancement of human ability to progress. At the very beginning, Adam and Eve were in a world that required work, but there was not a struggle between good and evil. I do not believe that their work in the garden of Eden was destroyed by nature. For example, the flowers they planted were not taken over by weeds. The dog they had as their pet was not killed by another animal, and it did not run out of the house, causing Adam to chase after him for twenty minutes.

But this world was suddenly taken away when Adam rejected a simple regulation. From that point on, humankind learned that what Adam was told not to seek resulted in destruction. As a result, humankind was destroyed—with the exception of Noah and his family and male and female of all creatures. All others were destroyed, but Noah alone was allowed to restart or restore human continuity with God and the universe.

But humankind again attempted to do that which was not part of our purpose—to believe it could establish itself as lord of the universe. The result was the dispersion of humankind by God via the creation of different languages. This setback of human progressive actions resulted in another attempt to gain superiority. This new idea was to replace God's role as leader and Creator with their own perspective of what good should be. They created idols to guide and inspire themselves. But God again said, "No, I'm not going to share My role as Creator and sustainer." So, He challenged the priests of the idol gods. You can read this in Kings 18. This challenge technically ended idol worship.

But humankind was not finished because next, humans developed the scientific ideas expressed in philosophy. Written ideas were designed to replace the teachings of God by the study of nature. Humankind believed it could explain the existence and nature of people by studying what individuals had done and what they had accomplished. Again, God said, "Not good enough," and so He organized His purpose by writing the theological understanding of God and humankind.

Individuals then came up with the theories stated in psychology, with the purpose of giving humankind inspiration to advance and explain human weaknesses by labeling them as illnesses. God brought forward men like Norman Vincent Peale, who explained what God already had laid out—how we can find inspiration and guidance for a joyful life. With the help of theology and psychology, we can find encouragement and enlightenment to achieve our goals. The listing of our weaknesses and creating medicines for mental illnesses does help us in many ways, but in many cases, this is not sufficient to bring about full recovery. Because I have worked in a mental and physical health institution for the handicapped, I realize that help via our limited abilities will never complete the process of healing for many individuals, not until Christ Himself can give us all healthy mental and physical bodies.

I believe that if individuals would combine medicine with a personal willingness to submit themselves to the hands of God and accept His grace, mass tragedies would not be happening in the manner that appears to be so prevalent. The mass killings that we have experienced in the past years have been blamed on mental illness or were given some obscure name, like Trump-phobia. The truth is that almost all the tragedies were the result of sin—the action of Satan working in and with individuals.

All of these progressive steps are attempts to replace God, to make humans equal with God, and to advance humankind's self-improvement by going from God being King to appointing a human as king. We went from a Jewish nation to a Christian nation and now to a Judeo-Christian nation. All these progressive improvements have brought humankind to its greatest capabilities. So, just as we have run out of new territory and have achieved the best of community, living with the achievements of the Judeo-Christian society, we now have achieved the ultimate of our intellectual capacity. We have evolved from mystical, superstitious thinking to the science of philosophy and psychology. As Swiss Reformed theologian Emil Brunner wrote in *The Divine Imperative*:

It is the nature of the Ego, or of the self, that it consists not only of its creative powers, but also of its view of its own nature, and of the aim of self-realization which it sets before itself. (1937,170)

These thoughts expressed by Danish theologian Soren Kierkegaard are contrary to the basic thinking of Christians, who adhere to the idea that the ego brought humans into sin in the first place. Following this thought, if man chooses to live with this as a basis for his actions, then:

he chooses to run directly to the purpose for which he was created—that is if he plans his life apart from God, basing all on his own independent existence he loses both his hopes of self-realization, and his freedom. (Brunner 1937. 170)

If we, as citizens of this nation, which has the best that humans have been able to achieve, now decide to base our way of life on our own thinking—on our "own independent existence"—we will lose not only our self-realization but also the freedoms that God has created for us.

I believe that the Reformation was the major steppingstone toward the advancement of our living together with the freedom never before experienced. This was the period when, for the first time, we united the principles of the Old and New Testaments.

With this progressive movement forward, the Pilgrims came to the New World and established communities based on ideas expressed in the Old and New Testaments. The result of this new way of understanding scripture was a nation that evolved for the first time in human history; it was created and recognized as a Judeo-Christian nation or society.

As we compare and contrast the development of both the

Jewish nation and the Christian nations, we must recognize similar characteristics in their stages of development. We can compare the advancing nature of God using "miracles." When Joshua was confronted with the walls of Jericho, the Lord came to him and told him to march around the city once a day for six days. On the seventh day, his army, and priests, with the ark of the covenant, was to march around the city seven times. Then, everyone was to yell, at which point the walls would fall. (You can read this story in Joshua 6.) This took place about forty years after the people walked through the Red Sea.

Now let's turn to the War of 1812, which happened about thirty years after America's independence. We have a number of miracles to consider. The first was the saving of Washington, DC. Although the capital was destroyed, the city itself was saved by a mighty storm. Winds that were strong enough to move cannons compelled the British to forgo burning down the city.

The second miracle occurred when the captain of a British war ship, Captain Lockyer, met with the notorious pirate Jean Lafitte, hoping to get Lafitte to join the British against the Americans. The miracle was that Lafitte, using deception, refused Lockyer's offer and gave support to Andrew Jackson.

Then we have the famous story of Francis Scott Key, who woke up on September 17, 1814, to see the Stars and Strips still flying over Fort McHenry and wrote our national anthem, "The Star-Spangled Banner." (You can read more about these magnificent stories in *Andrew Jackson and the Miracle of New Orleans* by Brian Kilmeade and Don Yaeger.

How does this affect us? I believe this leads us to a very fundamental reality—that the United States of America is the John the Baptist of nations, a nation that was created as the last nation. God has run out of new land. We are also a nation created to be in union with God's attempt to establish Himself as King and to give us laws that can unite and guide us as people.

He gave us the individual personal gift of Jesus Christ and the help of the Holy Spirit. What else, then, can there be for humankind? If the story of the tower of Babel (Genesis 11:1–9) is any indication, settling on a planet out in the heavens will not be achieved, although I believe it something we should strive to accomplish, just as we must continue to fight to keep what we have.

Chapter 3

I believe that Jesus Christ, with the authority of God, His Father, started organizing this nation soon after the final fall of Israel and the temple. (Of course, it was God's plan before He created the world.) The result is that this nation was created and has the purpose of being the John the Baptist of nations. The book *Promise and Deliverance* by S. G. De Graaf explains the purpose of God's bringing John into the world. De Graaf's ideas are based on Luke 1:1–25, 57–80.

First, John was to "prepare the people for the coming of the Lord." With regard to the United States, God has prepared us with a long secular history of political, social, religious, and governmental experiments. The trials, along with incorporating Old and New Testament biblical teachings, allowed our forefathers to develop ideals expressed in our governing principles. Just like John being filled with the Holy Spirit from the moment of conception, God has given us a valid foundation to carry our (His) task forward. The foundation was acquired by studying history and political science and by reading the holy Word, plus the personal experience of our forefathers—for example, living under the rule of a king. I believe the Declaration of Independence, the US Constitution, and the Bill of Rights highlight the preparation for our nation and the nations to come.

Second, John's parents were instructed that John was not to drink any wine or strong drink as a sign that he did not receive any strength from this earth but only from God. This was done so people would learn to trust in God, rather than in the man himself. This element of trust in God can be seen by the founding fathers learning and discarding many of the social behaviors and teachings of Europe and the history of prior nations and their own history. These lessons were signs that were enlightened from God so that the people could act in faith and with trust in God. Even though these documents and wars were not perfect, they do offer us reasons to believe and trust in God's authorship, and as such, we should learn to trust in God.

Third, just as sin separates people from God's grace, John's struggle was to bring about a conversion of the people for the coming of the Lord Jesus Christ. So, it is with us today; as citizens of the United States, we, too, struggle to bring about a conversion for the nations of the world and their citizens. God has given us, for the first time in the history of humankind, things that can give us a strong and demanding leadership in our struggle. Study of history shows us that our founding fathers struggled with the principle of socialism versus republicanism, government control of society versus individualism, and kings that rule as dictators versus representatives expressing the freedom and choice of laws from the people.

The hard truth is that God guided the men to the freedoms we have, and for us to convert to any other form of governing is to reject what God created and ordained. Our form of leadership was created after many debates. Debates were often bitter, but even when they were divisive, the debates were recognized as necessary to form a united nation. Those debates were done openly, not in secret behind locked doors, in rooms filled with fear that the secrets would become known.

I cannot help but reflect on unity or grace that is demonstrated in today's America. After the trial and guilty verdict of former

Minneapolis police officer Derek Chauvin, many Left political advocates went to Minneapolis to advocate for more diversity. US Representative Maxine Waters from California went to Minneapolis with taxpayer-paid security guards to tell rioters, who were already prepared for any excuse to burn the city, that they needed to be more confrontational and be noticed. President Biden said that more needed to be done to eliminate racism in our country, but he failed to suggest ways to unite us.

Let's consider other qualifications, such as names. The name *John* means "the Lord is gracious." John was to introduce the kingdom of grace brought about by Jesus. No other nation up to the time our forefathers had chosen the words *United States*. United was never conceived or used as a name. United represents the idea of people (states) being together with one purpose. It's not much of a stretch to say that people being united cannot be united without having grace to unite us.

Remember that John's world was not in grace; he was introducing it to the world. As such, we as a nation are not in a state of complete union (grace), but we have demonstrated the possibilities of being united and free, so much so that millions have already come, and many others desire to come—at least this was true until the current events of lies, and half-truths became so prevalent today. Americans have always been debaters; it's the principal characteristic of a republican government and a major point of misunderstanding in many nations. I believe, however, that the division and the debates have become more personal since the Clinton administration and were greatly advanced with the Obama administration. History tells us that many presidential campaigns were harsh and very bitter. President Lincoln was confronted with bitter threats, but he was fighting to keep the nation united.

We have come to some very divisive ideas. Never before have generations been indoctrinated with the socialism and communism that can be found in our colleges and universities today—ideas that are so contrary to our founding principles; ideas that are based on lies, race, and hate; ideas that promote division and destruction; and ideas that contradict the principle of grace of unity.

Because John did not gain strength from the earth but from the Holy Spirit, people "learned to trust again in their God." It was through this "struggle" (learning to trust in God) that John was able to convert some, who then followed Jesus. Those who study and understand our history likely will acknowledge God's creative power. Our forefathers studied history and philosophy, both social and political sciences, and thus created a nation with bicameral houses of legislature and division of powers (executive, judicial, and legislative), as well as writing and accepting such documents as the Declaration of Independence, the Constitution, and the Bill of Rights. We therefore have the material to bring the conversion to other nations and to recognize our nation as being the John the Baptist of nations.

At this time in the history of our nation, we are confronted with the reality of unbelief. Just as Zechariah, the father of John, did not believe that he and his wife, Elizabeth, could have a child because of their advanced ages, we now have people who act in total unbelief. They refuse to accept that we are a nation of grace, a nation created to demonstrate and offer unity and grace. Because Zechariah did not believe, God punished him by making him dumb until the child was born.

Are we now being led into a time of punishment? As of this writing, we have lost, by the stroke of a pen, the "free capitalism" with the ending of the gas line. We have lost security for American citizens with the opening of the southern borders. We have lost free speech with corporate actions by the closing of Twitter accounts of Donald Trump and many of his advocates. God did restore Zechariah's speech after he discovered how horrible his sin was.

So, too, is it possible for them to recognize their sins so that God might give us grace again and give those who don't agree with the policies of the Left to have the right to express their opinions.

I urgently plead that we all need to continue to do what God has given us the ability to do. Our talents and positions will allow us to convince God to give us a second chance. Because as history shows, we are out of new territory, and we are living in the best possible governing arrangement that we have available (the union of the Old Testament and New Testament, God as King, and Christ advising us to form a new type of government). We need to vote to keep our Constitution and the freedoms and rights it guarantees.

So, what happened to John the Baptist? People who sought their own desires and vengeance, rather than accepting what God desired from them, brought about John's imprisonment and death. The result was that after using the young daughter of the king's wife, John was beheaded. As individuals and as members of this nation, will we excuse the killing of unborn children so that our lives will somehow be better? Are we willing to sacrifice the fundamental principle of life, liberty, and justice for those who are aborted so we can have more for ourselves?

Turning to Luke 7:24, we see that Jesus talked to the crowd about John. He asked, "Who did you go out to see?" Biblical scholar F. F. Bruce made the following observation in his *New Testament History*:

> The multitudes which flocked to the Jordan valley to hear him from all parts of Palestine did so because men recognized in his preaching a note of authority the like of which had not been heard in Israel for centuries: "all held that John was a real prophet" (Mark 11:32). (1972, 154)

Why did people come to the New World? Originally, they came to see and experience something the world had not heard of. No one could believe that citizens of a nation could tell their government what it could or could not do. People have come to the United States and found freedom that was never before experienced in the history of nations.

Jesus continued, "Did you find him weak as a reed, moved by every breath of wind?"

In reading F. F. Bruce's *New Testament History*, we begin to realize the new teachings that John was introducing:

> It is not as a disciple of any other Teacher of Righteousness, but as a new teacher of righteousness with his own following of disciples, that we know the historical John the Baptist. (1972, 154)

In this New World, people found a nation, not as a disciple or follower of other nations but secure in its own written laws, with individual rights guaranteed by our Bill of Rights. They found they had the right to go where they wanted and to do what they believed was right for them, and they had the right to say what was best for them and to worship as they believed.

In Luke 7:29, Jesus also said, "Were you looking for a prophet? Yes, and he is more than a prophet." Were the people who came to the New World looking for a nation of Judeo-Christian principles? For most, the answer probably was no, but they found a nation free from any religious domination, and they had the freedom to express their thoughts without fear and to create their own business or work where they wanted.

> I tell you, of all who have ever lived, none is greater
> than John. (Luke 7:30)

I believe that today, Jesus would say, I tell you that of all nations that have ever existed, none is greater than the United States, yet the most insignificant nation in the kingdom of God is greater than the USA.

I'd like to express one more thought from F. F. Bruce: "The baptism of John was a new thing in Israel" (55). The religious leaders were not impressed. "They had their own ideas of what constituted the way of righteousness" (1972, 158).

So, too, many in other nations are not impressed with our form of government and our political exercises for governing, but our system, based on Judeo-Christian principles, has created a nation that no one has been capable of creating. The truth is, however, that we will not be able to continue without God and His blessings.

Chapter 4

How shall I describe this generation? ...They are like a group of children playing a game in the public square. They complain to their friends.

—Luke 7:31–32

Today, people act like children, distorting the truth, such as changing emails and changing dates of emails, like what was done for the second impeachment trial of former president Trump. They refused to tell the whole story by omitting parts of statements or not showing the complete videos used during the impeachment trial. They also changed the rules in the middle of the game, such as changing voter laws without state ratification just before voting began in 2020. Reflecting more on this generation, Herman Ridderbos, in his book *Paul: An Outline of His Theology*, writes concerning Paul's idea of history and the "falling away" and the "mystery of godlessness":

> What is meant by this is that the wonders of the lawless one has a mendacious, deceitful purpose they lead men astray...Those who are already on the road to ruin are totally beguiled and misled by the deceptive delusions of God's arrogant adversary and the manifestations of his power. (1975, 526)

This generation has accepted God's arrogant adversary's and their deceptive delusions of socialism and communism. To advance the understanding of Paul's concept of the future in 2 Thessalonians 2, we get a limited view of the expectation of the future. Ridderbos writes:

> The limitation of clarity, of concrete knowledge of the possibility of being able to survey history in its factual progress ... For the knowledge of the prophet is something other than sharing in divine omniscience. Nevertheless, this prophecy joins the kingdom of God with history, and it teaches us to see history under the decisive points of view. (1975, 528)

The earliest colonists already realized that Christianity shows the vast extent of evil in humans. The colonist saw "his own guilt condemned, takes it really upon himself; and he alone knows that in his guilt he is united with the whole of humanity" (Brunner, 57). They realized that this guilt brought them to the cross.

> For the word of the Cross is the word of reconciliation and forgiveness, and as such is the foundation for, and the source of, a new active existence (Brunner, 1937, 57)

It was this new foundation—the recognition of God's adversary—that is evil, as well as the concrete knowledge of history and the knowledge of the prophets who carried them into the new existence. The knowledge of the prophets was the result of the Reformation. The combination of these thoughts brought the Pilgrims to the New World and eventually sent many Americans out into the world as missionaries. The word of reconciliation and forgiveness gave them the foundation to build a society that allowed for freedom and justice for all.

The fact that this movement west to the New World happened almost a century after the Reformation resulted in altering the individualism of the New Testament to incorporate the principles of the Old Testament, which is the idea that God began with the community, a nation. This acknowledgement of how individual freedom from evil through the Word of the cross is in union with God. It is this union with God that incorporates the individual with the King, Jesus Christ, and with their community and church and the new towns—and eventually a "new" nation. The true good of the cross, therefore, "[lies] only in the power of God and not in that of man: that no other human goodness and good conduct exists save that which is based on the free gift of God" (Brunner, 1937, 58).

It then follows that from the free gift from God (the gift of Jesus Christ), our forefathers realized that to place these free gifts into the realm of a king or queen was to subject our true freedom to the whims of one individual. The concept of granting our freedom to a committee, either elected or appointed, was also giving away our rights. Thus, our founders not only developed a form of government that separated authority but also listed certain rights that no other human has a right to take from us: freedom of speech, to peacefully congregate, to worship free of government or other human regulations. The list goes on in the Bill of Rights. It was the power of God and the separation of authority that our forefathers found to be good, and *good* would be to allow the freedom of Christ, as expressed in each person through private voting in free elections.

Let's consider a perspective from Herman Ridderbos in *Paul: An Outline of His Theology*:

What established the connection between life before and after the resurrection and what "passes over" from the one into the other is the Spirit and being under the ruler ship of the Spirit. In so far as man is flesh and blood, he will not inherit the kingdom of God (1 Cor. 15:30), but the kingdom of God is never the less already present in righteousness, peace, and joy through the Holy Spirit (Rom. 14:17), what "abides" is faith, hope, and love (1 Cor. 13:13). (1975, 551)

From this perspective, our forefathers and those who followed them were living after the Resurrection of Christ but before the resurrection of our bodies, and as such, they lived in the present kingdom of God. Although we have not lived the perfect life, we are living in a world of grace. Perhaps we need to admit that we do abominable acts at times, but that does not negate the righteousness, peace, and joy that we seek with the help of the Holy Spirit. Even though we have failed in many ways, we also have achieved in many ways in faith, hope, and love. Millions of people around the world sought and sacrificed to get here. Therefore, God created our nation as a John the Baptist of nations, laying a foundation for the kingdom of Christ that will follow the Antichrist.

I often wonder what kind of kingdom Christ will create and will rule for a thousand years. I imagine it will be a more perfect democratic republic. It will be made better than we have today because Christ will have the ability and authority, granted to Him from God, to eliminate any thought of those who wish to destroy what He has created. If He were here today, anyone attempting to censor our freedom of speech—including the social media, the House of Representatives or Senate committees, or any executive orders or corporate policies—would be done away and their ideas erased from our memories. Those who attempt to limit or do away with our freedom of religion, including scientists who spread fear of assembling in worship, will have no voices to spread their destruction. Their voices will be silenced not out of fear, but because of love.

We are a nation that God created, giving us the best, He has to offer. But it is also a nation that must prepare for what will follow. If I understand the events of world progression, we will be followed by the Antichrist, in which the recent events of anguish, sorrow, and sin will seem like child's play. It will get so terrible that if God does not stop the Antichrist, his actions and policies will bring the world to an end.

Chapter 5

As in mystery movies and television programs, where cops say they don't believe in coincidence, I cannot believe it was a coincidence that it took me more than five years to finish reading *Paul: An Outline of His Theology*. Today, I read the final chapter, which offered the theological perspectives of Paul's writings from almost two thousand years ago. Considering human development that has brought us to where we are today and considering the ideas for the future, I need to express what I believe are God's three priorities for this world.

I believe the first priority is the salvation of the individual. This has already been accomplished and is summed up in first of two most profound statements by Jesus. The first statement was made in response to a question asked by His disciples: "How is it possible for us to enter into the kingdom of heaven?" Jesus responded, "No one comes to the Father except through me." We might not understand the simplicity of this concept, or maybe we don't want to humble ourselves to such simplicity. But that doesn't change the reality of God's offer. Believe in Jesus Christ—it is that simple.

As we consider this offer of individual salvation—that all we need to do is accept Christ—we cannot ignore the second of the most profound statements, in which, I believe, Christ referred to the final result of humankind. The question was, "Who will be saved?" (that is, who will be allowed into the kingdom of heaven?).

His response was, "Thousands will be saved." Doesn't that sound magnificent, wonderful, and something to rejoice about?

I think of the stadiums full of people, gathered to hear Dr. Billy Graham proclaim the salvation in Jesus Christ, and the more recent events of thousands who gathered to hear Donald J. Trump tell us about how to make America great again.

But Christ did not end his statement with "Thousands will be saved." He then said, "But generations will be left standing outside the gate crying 'why not me Lord, why not me.'" Think of it— thousands versus hundreds of millions, if not billions (generations). The term He used was *thousands*, compared to generations. I emotionally fall to my knees and thank God that I am one of the thousands.

I recall a story that Dr. Hageman told the students in his class on church liturgy. He told us about a book he had in his library that was made up of stories from articles that were discovered in a town in India—articles that someone had written and posted on a community board in town. One of the articles, which was believed to have been written about AD 20, told of a young Hebrew man by the name of Jesus (English translation), who came into town. He was recorded to have healed many sick people and performed other miracles. He also told the people that there was only one God who created the world and who was watching over them.

I can hear the skeptics saying that is ridiculous; Christ's ministry was roughly within a hundred-mile radius of Jerusalem. The reality of the time was that a number of trade caravans traveled from Jerusalem to India, trading spices and cloth and other goods. Each caravan made at least two trips each year, so all Jesus had to do was hitch a ride or walk along with them. The bottom line was that Jesus knew more about the number of people in the world than the area around Jerusalem; as such, He was well aware of what he was implying.

The second priority that God has for humankind is the family. We can follow the significance of the family even before the written laws from Moses. Consider the promise made to Abraham that he would be the father of nations, then the history of the generations that followed Abraham. Then there are the laws telling us to honor our mother and father, plus other actions that form a family. The importance of family is reflected in the listing of the generations by Matthew, concluding with the birth of Christ.

Unfortunately, like the individuals who were not able to accept God's gift of Christ, there are those who try to destroy the family. I heard a message from Dr. James Stackpole in Flatbush, New York, many years ago. He said that the social and economic issues of society have brought about the destruction of the family and the development of single parenting, with the father absent and many children being raised by babysitters or nannies. He suggested that we need to redefine what family is. Respectfully, I believe we cannot redefine that which God has ordained. We clearly need to recognize the added destruction of the family with the millions of abortions taking place in America today. All this reflects the reality of the destruction of the family; it is, in fact, the basis for destroying the third and final priority that God has for humankind.

This final priority is the nation. We see this concept as the creation of a way by which individuals can come together and live-in small towns and large cities. We can form neighborhoods and workplaces, but nations are created with individuals. I believe the final project that God has for humankind is that we will become members of His kingdom.

> The fundamental thought of all Paul's preaching of salvation is that they [people] do not receive this [kingdom] otherwise than in communion with Christ that they have been chosen in him from

before the foundation of the world to live holy and
blameless lives before God and to be conformed
to his image that he might be the firstborn among
many brethren (Ephesians 1:4; Romans 8:29ff)
(Ridderbos: Paul An Outline of His Theology,
1975, p. 560.)

The salvation that Paul referred to is the individual, but does
this mean that we cannot apply this to the continuing existence
of any nation, as long as that nation is in communion with Christ,
blameless before God, conformed to His image, and the firstborn
among nations? If a nation was created to be conformed to God's
image, would there be a reason why God would destroy such a
nation? After all, God did promise the people of his first nation that
He would be their King as long as they lived lives that corresponded
to His expectations. It was obvious that He did not expect sinless
individuals. We see this from the story of God expressing His
anger and threatening to destroy the people but then changing
His mind after Moses argued with God. Nations are a project that
God desires for the people that He has created, and He will do
everything possible to work with us.

Ridderbos describes Paul's final thought concerning Christ's
act of redemption:

Redemption carried out by Christ is at the fore.
The purpose for which he was sent by God (cf. e.g.,
Rom 8:3ff.; Gal 4:4f.) and for which he has been
invested with divine authority will then have been
attained. (1975, 560–561)

The redemption that Christ carried out was culminated on
the cross and in the victory over death, redeeming humans to be
free from sin.

For this is the word in which Christ's power and commission are described: "he [God] has put all things in subjection under his [Christ] feet" (I Cor. 15: 25-27) ... But this word also implies that God was himself the great Initiator and Authorizer and that therefore the state of perfection cannot be spoken before God himself again fills all things with his glorious presence (vv. 27b-28). The manner in which the consummation of his work Christ is thereby made subordinate to the Father is ... a specific aspect of the great future. (Ridderbos, 1975, 561)

I firmly believe that since the time and works of Christ, God, as the great initiator, has spoken and created a new nation, established in a new world. Let's take a bird's-eye view of history and some acts of God. After the Resurrection of Christ, God created His church. With the help of Paul and the other disciples, the church was spread throughout the world. As time passed, the church became the most powerful and influential organization the world had witnessed. The problem was that it developed into an organization dominated by one person. Although the pope always has been ordained by God, he always has been a man. As time moved on, some of the popes who led the church followed their human desires and became corrupt, as human activities often become. But I believe that one major issue displeased God the most—that the church fulfilled only part of what God intended. Christ did not rule out the teachings of the Old Testament. He did not abandon the promise God made to Abraham, so Christ did not abolish the Jews. The early church, however, basically did so. Although the scholars and theologians tied the Old Testament with the New Testament, the local priests ignored the Old Testament and the way in which it was to help direct the lives of the people in the congregations.

This began the next chapter of God's creation of history—the reorganization of the church. With the advancement of the Reformation, the church began teaching lessons from the Old Testament for the first time. Because of this new perspective in Christianity, people incorporated thoughts and ideas into their thinking and desires for a better form of living.

With this progressive development of understanding the total picture of God's message, individuals moved west to the New World, where they found a society that was not as developed as in the old world. The new arrivals planned for major changes from the old world, but they were unable to clearly relate to the Native Americans and so major problems developed. The difference between the two cultures is a complicated topic and not part of this summary view of history. Both sides have arguments as to why things developed as they did, but the lack of mutual understanding and not being able to communicate with each other resulted in wars and mistrust from both parties.

The ultimate result was that the newcomers who arrived here brought the updated version of what it meant to live together as a new community. History shows people uniting Old and New Testament principles to govern their existence. They made many errors, but the final establishment was revolutionary and resulted in a new, never-before-tested concept of government. This "new" form, however, was actually developed in Israel during the time of judges, and this new set of laws and organization was soon recognized as a Judeo-Christian society. This phase of human history was important, and it is equally important that we understand what it means for us today.

First, we must realize that if we reject what God has given us, we will be signing the death warrant for our nation and for the entire world. Remember that after Christians moved west, there was no longer any new western territory to which they could move, so there was little option for what was next. Also, humankind rejected the first nation that God created and then failed to comply with or understand God's intentions for the "Christian" nations, so what will be available to us if we deliberately mess up this Judeo-Christian nation? The prime examples of governments available, other than ours, are the socialist or communist attempts at utopia, and their success was mass murders, stripping of individual success and the freedom to strive for their personal success, results in ultimate failure.

Chapter 6

Here are a few examples of how this nation is being destroyed: During his speech following his promise to uphold the Constitution, President Biden promised to work to unite this nation. Just hours later, he signed an executive order to stop the XL pipeline, eliminating thousands of good-paying construction jobs, not to mention the thousands of jobs related to the pipeline industry. In addition, the order will cause the price of gasoline at our pumps to go higher and higher and will increase an unknown numbers of trucks to haul oil on our highways. Truck accidents and rail accidents can cause immense damage due to oil spills, damaged property, and deaths. The rail system is not accident-free.

At approximately the same time, the president signed another executive bill. After promising safety improvements and renewed efforts to fight the drug problem, he stopped construction of the southern border wall and opened the border to all illegal invaders (including drug traffickers supported by his friends in China, sex traffickers, and all sorts of criminal elements—I'm thinking of MS-13 members). He ignored the health and safety of the American citizens with this action by allowing individuals to enter the country with the COVID-19 virus and then transporting them by bus and plane to cities of their choice without the required isolation time. Many more policy changes reflect the destruction to our Constitution and our Bill of Rights, as they were designed by our forefathers.

We must not accept what the media has done for the past five years—distorting the truth by not reporting the total reality of Trump's actions and the efforts of many on the Right to bring justice and unity. We cannot accept that social media has censored Trump and many other conservatives. We must not adhere to the idea that hardworking, honest Americans across this land have to fork out billions of our tax dollars to pay for the stupid, corrupt Democrats, who have destroyed California, New York, and Minnesota, as well as Chicago, Portland, Seattle, and the other Left-ruled cities. It's been reported that almost 30 percent of Democrats who were interviewed said that if they had heard about Hunter Biden's relationships and business dealing in Ukraine and China, they would have voted for Trump. In understanding the advancement of the political and corporate destructive moves in our society, Christians around the world should also recognize and be aware of other signs in these times in which we are living.

Many years ago (more than I care to admit), I attended a Baptist church—the city in which I was working did not have a congregation of the denomination I'd grown up attending, and my mom was a Baptist until she married my dad. The experience taught me the truth—that Christians are people who all have a love for Christ, but they also have differences that may result in stubborn separations. As I see it, within a short time we may have to ignore these differences so we can find comfort in each other.

What I remember about that Baptist church, first and foremost, was the minister giving a series of sermons on biblical miracles. He said that the ten plagues that confronted the Egyptians in God's actions to free His people could be explained from a scientific or natural viewpoint. What I found most interesting, however, was his final question: how will it be possible for those of us on this side of the world to see the glorious return of Christ that will take place on the other side of the globe? (This series of sermons took place before there was satellite television, the internet, or cell phones.) The pastor's answer to that question was from a Christian Science perspective—that under the right conditions, the earth's atmosphere can create a mirror effect.

I don't disagree with that thought, but I have a much simpler explanation which copies the story of the ten plagues; that is, that the ten plagues had an appearance of being natural. I believe we will see Christ's glorious return with His host of angels, and we will see it in living color. We have gone out into the world and spread the gospel to all nations, and we also have introduced the world to satellite communications. Some individuals in remote areas of the world may not have satellite communications, but I'll bet they know someone who does. It's like the Bruce Willis movie *Armageddon*, in which the entire world knew about and was watching for the asteroid that would wipe out all of humankind. So, too, will every television network have twenty-four-hour coverage of Christ and his angels as they descend to the earth. Consider the issues of famine, earthquakes, floods, pestilence, wars, and rumors of wars. Regardless of where these things happen, in all locations around the world, we certainly hear about them and see them every day.

Those who predict the end of the world due to climate change are correct, except that it will not happen because of temperature changes. You can be assured that when our televisions show the coming of Christ, those who claim the end will be from climate change will laugh and ridicule those who recognize it as being Christ. In addition, they'll cry for the complete destruction of this invasion via the use of nuclear weapons. Following Christ's glorious return, God will end the reign of the Antichrist and will establish His kingdom that will last for a thousand years. I'll argue that our Constitution and Bill of Rights are preliminary factors in the governing principles that Christ will establish.

Does this mean that we give up hope? Do we stop fighting for what we have? No. By *fighting*, I mean doing everything we can to cling to our faith, our hope, and our Constitution. Christ continued His mission, knowing what was going to happen in Jerusalem, knowing He was going to the cross. We, too, must continue to confront those who are trying to rid us of what God created for us.

In relation to our bringing history to an end, we also need to consider the blessings we have been allowed to create for ourselves. We know how satellite television, cell phones, and the internet could help Christ reveal His glorious return, but let's look at the problems these same progressive instruments could cause. Although these tools allow for instant exchange of ideas and news updates, they also create individual isolation issues. Parents may not take care of their children because they are so involved with television, with telephone conversations with maybe an adulterous friend, or with games on the internet—or worse, pornography. Children also keep their minds and attention on these tools of communication and ignore physical contact and conversations with other individuals, thus distorting their social growth and interactions. All these actions are destructive to individuals and their psychological well-being, but there is a far greater problem. These instruments of social advancement are a hindrance to individuals' relationships with God. In the Ten Commandments, God admits that he is a jealous God and that He will destroy anything that comes between Him and His people.

I believe that all things created are good, so will God actually destroy the modern-day social media and communication, or will he improve the system so we can use it, as it has potential?

As we think about signs that reflect how we are bringing ourselves to the brink of destruction, let's consider how John the Baptist questioned his role. He was to help bring about the new world, which he knew Christ would bring to the chosen people of God, but he probably wondered why he was locked up in jail.

His physical state was the result of his criticizing Herod (you can read about this in Luke 3). The real issue for John, however, was if he had been right about his message to the people. He then asked some friends to find Jesus to get some clarification before his life was ended.

Many also are wondering about their futures. Throughout the summer of 2020, we saw very disturbing events in our country. Many of us can remember the riots and protests of the 1960s, and many probably took part in those events, but I believe the actions in summer 2020 represent vastly different social issues. In the 1960s, social unrest was an attempt to change government policies so that Americans could return to the nation of peace rather than death. We asked why individuals had to die in a foreign land. The destruction of our communities and the killing of innocent citizens in the summer of 2020 was an attempt by evil people to destroy the very foundation of our nation. Antifa and the Black Lives Matter (BLM) movement both were created by hate and self-professing communist ideology. Individuals like US representatives Ilhan Omar and Alexandria Ocasio-Cortez and their friends all tried to abolish our Judeo-Christian society, the very thing thousands of people have died to create and sustain. Until 2021, thousands of people tried to get into our country through proper and legal channels, but I recently heard that people now are moving out and taking their citizenship with them. So Antifa and BLM are succeeding.

When we accept the ideas and principles defined in our Constitution and Bill of Rights, which are protected by our form of government by checks and balances, we, as individuals of this nation, experience what individuals who accept the cross and the Resurrection of Christ experience. We are changed. We become new people. I say this because of what I've heard individuals express when they become citizens. As a nation, the people find freedom;

with freedom, they find peace; with peace, they find joy. Granted, it's not the full freedom, peace, and joy that we will experience in heaven, but it is the best we can have while living in this world.

As individuals who accept the cross, our old desires die, and new desires fill us with excitement, challenging ideas, and the feeling of freedom to act. Notice how the legal immigrants who have come to the United States often create their own businesses. With these new principles of life as Christians—when we find that our thoughts are influenced by God—we recognize that the actions of those who attempt to destroy the foundation of our nation and those who develop a profound love, and a new way of thinking are both acts of individuals but granted by God. When John was in prison, he became convinced that Christ was the Messiah and that he, John, had to fade away. His newfound freedom and his acceptance of death to make room for Jesus both were decisions he made but was accepted by God. Similarly, even though we watch the news and see the destruction, we find peace in knowing God is very much aware of what is happening.

Emil Brunner described the actions of those seeking destruction, saying they were "permitted with this spirit of hostility to God" (174). The events that occurred in the summer of 2020 by those who attempted to destroy this nation happened because God permitted it, but it was not His desire. Through those acts of violence, we can witness what God did to His chosen nation and see that we then can be raised from the death of destruction, if we turn our ways. It is by faith that changes take place.

> Faith, since it means being in Christ, also means being a member in His body, life in the Christian community, union with those who belong to Him. (Brunner, 176)

Being in a Judeo-Christian society means following the founding principles outlined for us in the Constitution and the

Bill of Rights. To be raised in Christ is to be free from ourselves so we can be free for others. The totalitarian and socialistic forms of government take away this freedom. Followers of those forms, however, argue that their principles create sharing and equalization of wealth, but the reality is that the power needed to share and equalize is given to a few individuals, who dictate what, when, and how we must give. They also dictate what we must do to help create that which is needed to share. In other words, we have no freedom to seek our desires or to promote our abilities to create methods by which we can fulfill our needs and the needs of others.

To conclude this idea of being a member of the new society of freedom, let me refer again to Brunner's *The Divine Imperative*:

> To be a member and to be "holy" is the same thing;
> for both means to be dedicated to God, to be united
> with God, and therefore to be united with other
> men in fellowship. (177)

We are united, not by force from a dictated government but because we are in God. As in the church, Americans are called out as members of elected citizens, who have been given the privilege of living in this nation. Again, from Brunner:

> The new regard for personality is based upon this
> fact: that man, as an individual, knows that God is
> continually regarding him (individual) with favor,
> he knows for a certainty, in the deep and secret
> places of the soul, where he is alone with God, that
> God regards him thus. (p. 177-178)

This means that we know that God is controlling, creating, and bringing events to the conclusion that He has planned for us. The question is this: are we going to affirm or deny that the events that have taken place are acts of God? If we reject this premise, then we will live in fear, in anger, and in death, and even contemplate suicide. If, however, we accept the idea that God allowed all these events and they are part of His plan, then we will be able to live with the results. This does not mean we stop fighting, but it does mean we will continue to live.

Chapter 7

Let's turn to the sign of the pestilence that Christ refers to in relation to the signs of the end. In January 2020, the "China virus" (coronavirus) found its way to the United States. This was not an act created by God because I believe God never intends for His children to suffer. He does allow us, however, to self-destruct, and He uses our actions to awaken us to the reality of sin and forces us to consider what is happening.

The result of the coronavirus—in my opinion and in the opinions of many people—is that it has revealed our trust in God or our lack of trust. Recall that faith means being in Christ. Lack of faith means not being in Christ but attempting to be in ourselves. I won't reject the reality of what science has informed us. Our forefathers created this nation with the words of scripture and words of God but also through the study of science (philosophy, political science, and secular history). So, too, we need to listen to the medical doctors and the development of medicines and vaccines. The use of masks as protective gear is appropriate and demonstrates our faith that God has given us such devices for protection. But I believe that to keep wearing them when, scientifically, there is no need for them demonstrates our lack of faith in God's ability to protect us. For example, there was an uproar when Senator Ted Cruz removed his mask during a news conference, and a cameraman asked him to put his mask back on. Cruz's reply was essentially that if the man's faith did not give him assurance of protection, then he should move back. Cruz pointed out that all the individuals presents had been vaccinated or tested, and therefore there was no need for a mask. I would argue that Cruz's comment really said that we all are showing our lack of faith, not only lack of faith in science but lack of faith in God. I find it disturbing when I see people walking alone, or jogging in isolated areas, or driving down the street alone, yet they are wearing masks. To me, these are acts demonstrate disbelief, but they also insult God. In my mind, I don't know how people can claim to believe what Christ told us—that God sees the sparrow fall from the sky or that God has numbered the hairs on our heads—and then use masks when they are nowhere near any exposure or at risk of exposing others.

COVID-19 also has resulted in major shifts in social behavior. We need to evaluate the orders by our leaders to close down all gatherings, such as schools, restaurants, churches and other places of worship, weddings, and funerals. As I ponder the question of what this virus means for us and the implication it has in relation to the United States being a nation that offers the world a preview of what God intends for the future, I feel we must consider our freedoms. I believe we have established, so far, that as a nation, our citizens have had the greatest individual freedoms and the greatest citizen representation for self-rule. But we also have developed into a nation that has shown compelling disregard for God's desire to be our Lord and King. We have also neglected what God has given us by chasing foolish pipe dreams, as are expressed in the Green New Deal and the threatening prophecy of climate change. I believe the work done by the Chinese Communist Party and their deliberate releasing of the virus, not only to their own people but throughout the world, was a deliberate attempt to divide and then conquer the United States, as well as the other democracies in the world.

I believe there are two ways to understand the events of 2020–21.

We can approach the acts of those who created destruction and death throughout our cities, as well as the demands of the priest of the god of science to shut down communities (primarily those of Democratic leadership), as forces of division and confusion. This would bring us to a scene similar to that in Luke when Jesus was forced to carry his cross through the streets of Jerusalem.

> Great crowds trailed along behind, including many grief-stricken women. But Jesus turned and said to them. "Daughters of Jerusalem, don't weep for me, but weep for yourselves and for your children. For the days are coming when they will say, 'Fortunate indeed are the women who are childless ... People will beg the mountains to fall on them and the hills to bury them. (Luke 23:27–30)

We can view this virus and its effect on society as a death threat and the end of what we had before the invasion of this microscopic death weapon. Or we can understand that this is merely a sign of what can happen and what will happen. In other words, don't weep for what has happened in far-off big cities, but weep for us and for our children because if they succeed, we will be swept up into the destruction we have seen. As of now, we can see it as Zechariah described the results of the exiles being called home:

> After a period of glory, the Lord Almighty sent me against the nations who oppressed you. For he said,' Anyone who harms you harms my most precious possession. I will raise my fist to crush them, and their own slaves will plunder them. Then you will know that the Lord Almighty has sent me. (Zechariah 2:8–9)

I was told many years ago that no one except God knows when Christ will return. So, too, we cannot know which of the above choices is true. (People will beg the mountains to fall on them, or anyone who harms you harms my most precious possession.) I have to admit I pray it is the latter of the two and that we have time to repent and that, as Moses so long ago argued and saved his people, we, too, will be given more time.

To put the "Chinese virus" (coronavirus) into perspective with what it means to be a Christian, let's consider the following elements: Being a Christian is being saved by Christ's life (Romans 5:10) the Chinese virus means death. To be a Christian means having salvation with eternal glory (2 Timothy 2:10). It also means honor and immortality (Romans 2:7; 1 Corinthians 15:42ff; 2 Timothy 1:10). It means we have eternal glory (2 Corinthians 4:17) as well as being able to see things with perfect clarity (1 Corinthians 13:12). As Emil Brunner points out, we realize that the actions of those seeking destruction were "permitted with this spirit of hostility to God" (174). Those then seeking to destroy this nation have been permitted with their spirits of hostility so that we can learn the true meaning of the crucified Christ. We will know that the Lord Almighty has sent Christ. All these things—being saved by Christ, receiving eternal glory, honor, and immortality—give us qualifications of life and meaning (for life) from the gospel. We cannot bring all these to a complete understanding while we are yet in these bodies, but I believe America has offered its citizens these precious gifts better than any nation that humankind has ever enjoyed. I believe this because we are living in a nation created as a John the Baptist of nations.

It seems that I cannot place this issue aside. I was reading my nightly scripture when thoughts brought me back to my love for this nation and God's message and how it applies to me and to this country. I need to express the ideas that entered my mind after reading the scripture.

I reflected on some of my personal history, which began when I first felt that this nation was starting down the slippery slope to destruction. The first memory was the Clinton administration. I don't remember anything in particular, except maybe the immoral nature of his presidency and the general feeling of socialistic policies. I did not have the time and luxury of following politics closely at the time. Then the Bush years seemed to pass without much influence one way or another, except perhaps a general deterioration of our ethics, highlighted with the housing scandal and Wall Street corruption, resulting in government bailouts. I remember the strong leadership exhibited after the attacks on 9/11, but the action of the banks was a serious issue.

Then we had the Obama administration. I did not follow the political aspects of the election; I supported Obama primarily because he was African American and some of his idealistic ideas sounded reasonable, considering the corruption at the end of the Bush term. It wasn't until his second term that I realized some major issues were taking place that I felt were changing this nation in a negative way. I think the most concern I had was for his foreign policies, specifically with the Middle East and Israel. It involved the promise God made to Abraham: *I will bless those who bless you, and I will curse anyone who curses you.* Many people have been destroyed for ignoring that warning.

With the election of 2016, I was partially retired and could follow the political and personalities of the candidates, as well as become better educated about recent government activities. With the ride down the golden escalator and the speech by Donald J. Trump, I knew we were in for an exciting adventure. The number of Republican candidates increased the mystery of the campaign. The sometimes-harsh language and nonpolitically correct truths expressed by Mr. Trump made Americans face the reality of what had happened in America. No presidential candidate or president had used such awakening expressions since Harry S. Truman, but the difference between the two was the timing of history. I believe Trump's words were directed to individual personal matters and the media. whereas Truman's words expressed political policies. Trump's words were expressed during the "political correctness" phenomenon and continued to the public interchanges and debates between Mr. Trump and Hillary Clinton. His harsh words against a woman caused many to question whether he had a gentlemanly attitude and a quality of presidential manners. The public did, however, realize that Hillary placed herself in the arena, and I believe we saw that her true desire was not for American citizens but for the power and personal gains the office can bring.

The second time I was spoken to in a clear and unmistakable way seems to summarize the whole of the presidential campaign of 2016. I was recovering from a stay in the hospital and watching a news commentary. The commentators were describing the differences between the two candidates with regard to the military. They said that Hillary's policy was to continue what President Obama had been doing, which was to ignore the true purpose of the military. His strategy had been to direct actions from the Pentagon, rather than allow generals in the field to make decisions. President Obama allowed the equipment to become old (our military planes dropped from the sky because of faulty parts). Others were arguing that Mr. Trump planned to rebuild the military and to leave the decisions of military action to the generals in the field. It was at this point that the Lord told me that if He wanted to destroy this nation, He could do it with either candidate. (Remember the statement that before I die, I will see the downfall of the United States.) I questioned how God could do what he had just said and then realized what He meant. If Hillary was elected, our enemies could, with little resistance, come in and take over. If Trump were to win the election, we would destroy ourselves from within.

Many might argue that at no time in our history has there been such harsh and divisive political and social upheaval from outside and inside the halls of government, but I believe that is not true. From the very beginning, our form of governing has resulted in major discord. Thomas Jefferson's campaign brought about bitter debates. President Abraham Lincoln's years were embattled with war. Andrew Jackson's presidential campaign also had harsh debates. I believe we could find angry and hateful rhetoric in virtually every presidential and many senatorial and congressional campaigns. But the real danger in today's world is the timing in history; more important, it's the quality of the mindset of the American citizens and our leaders (not specifically government representatives and workers but corporate and media leaders). I believe that because of abortion, the issue of mental illness, the so-called excuse for the mass murders, all are signs of moral decay. Whatever might have resulted in the 2016 election, God was aware of the situation into which America found herself, and that He had the situation under control.

Chapter 8

I would like to explain the procedure I've used for reading scripture recently. Some months ago, I decided to read the Bible from front to back, but when I had finished with Psalms and was into Proverbs, I missed reading Psalms, so I began reading from it but continued my reading of the Bible. Then, weeks later, I decided I wanted to include a study of Revelation (I had never read that book). So, I would read from Psalms, then read a section of scripture as I continued to complete the entire Bible, and I then added Revelation. After reading it several times I expanded my study of prophecy by turning back to the Old Testament books, beginning with Daniel. Now, I'm reading three segments each night—just my way of reading God's Word. I use this method because I do not like searching for thoughts that support my purposes. Tonight, I was reading from Luke 16, which relates the story Christ told of the rich man and Lazarus. I am by no means a rich man, nor am I dying from "open sores", so the story does not have a direct personal impact on me. I realized, however, a direct correlation with modern-day corporate leaders and the average American citizen. I'm not saying that modern corporate leaders are any different from previous generations—for example, the railroad and steel giants during Teddy Roosevelt's days—but what makes today's leaders unique is the timing and the direct attack against our God-given rights.

First, there is the reality of corporate media, which not only censored Donald Trump but also many other conservative men and women. There is also the issue of major news organizations deliberately deceiving American citizens, denying them of their right to know the whole and truthful facts of events. When editors edit out complete statements or fail to broadcast entire speeches, they are taking away our right to have all the information we need to make righteous decisions, such as when the media refused to properly disclose the true developments of the many riots that took place during the summer of 2020.

Comparing the destruction that took place by Communist supporters and the hundreds of millions of dollars in damages in cities throughout the United States to the one incident in the Capitol building is like dogs licking the open sores of the beggar; it's like the media licking the minor issues of what took place at the Capitol but totally ignoring the destruction and deaths of the riots in our cities during the summer of 2020.

I turned to the Old Testament and read in the book of Habakkuk. As I quote from the scripture that follows, I will interject my thoughts from current events. "How long O Lord, must I call for help?" (Habakkuk 1:2). I am not so ignorant as to not acknowledge that this cry might be expressed by both sides, Democrats and Republicans. According to reports, many on the Left cried when Mr. Trump won the election in 2016, but from all evidence, their cries were not for the "beggars" (refer to Luke 16); their concerns were for their loss of power, wealth, and control, whereas now, the Right sees the rights and freedoms that are being taking away by the Left—the God-given rights and freedoms guaranteed in our Construction and Bill of Rights. I'll let you choose which issue has merit to cry to the Lord. On second thought I believe God does not want you to have that choice, because I cannot believe God would respond to the cry of someone losing power, wealth, and control by taking those same rights and freedoms from other citizens.

"Wherever I look, I see destruction and violence. I am surrounded by people who love to argue and fight" (Habakkuk 1:3). We "beggars," the deplorables, recall the nightly news during the summer of 2020 that reported the burning of businesses and government buildings in many Democratic-controlled cities and the killings (by police but much more by gangs in poor neighborhoods; children and babies hit by stray bullets). We constantly hear of violence instigated by Antifa and BLM members, of murder and rape by illegal invaders, of gangs distributing drugs that destroy young Americans and then are released from jail. "Everywhere I look, I see destruction."

"The law has become paralyzed and useless, and there is no justice given in the courts" (Habakkuk 1:4). Right now, there are governors and attorneys general who set free evil individuals who have destroyed the peace and joy of thousands of families, and "justice has become perverted" with bribes and trickery. Rich men, who have made their wealth from the citizens of this country, are using their wealth and power to buy judges, governors, and attorneys general so there is no justice for innocent citizens; this idea is incomprehensible. No wonder it is easier for a camel to go through the eye of a needle than for a rich man to get into heaven.

Habakkuk then voices his second complaint:

> O Lord my God, my Holy One, you who are eternal—is your plan in all of this to wipe us out? Surely not! O Lord our Rock, you have decreed the rise of these Babylonians [Chinese and the Chinese Communist Party] to punish and correct us for our terrible sins. You are perfectly just in this. But will you stand idly by while they swallow us up? Should you be silent while the wicked destroy people who are more righteous than they? (Habakkuk 1:12–13)

At the end of President Biden's first thirty days in office, I was watching *Justice with Judge Jeanine*. She listed lies that Americans had witnessed since Biden's inauguration. I followed up and listed the realities of his first thirty days:

1. The commentator pointed out that from Trump making America first, Biden was making us last.
2. Biden called for the end of the deportation of illegal immigrants (Fox News).
3. With migrants traveling to the United States, Biden said he was going to help all of us (*New York Post*).
4. Today's figures show three thousand migrants entering the US every day. (Obama said that one thousand per day was a crisis.)
5. Biden reinstated the catch-and-release order, allowing MS-13 gang members, drug cartels, and sex traffickers to freely do their thing.
6. Biden's roll-back of migrants-remaining-in-Mexico policy need not wait for vetting process (CBS News).
7. Biden stopped the border wall construction (executive order).
8. Adding to the huge pandemic concern, Americans were told to stay home, people were not allowed in restaurants, teachers were not allowed to teach in public schools (primarily in Democratic cities), and illegal immigrants were allowed into the country without COVID testing.
9. Eleven thousand pipeline workers were laid off, not counting the jobs lost from related industries, like those making the pipes.
10. Because of the cancellation of said pipeline, gas prices went up sixty cents per gallon (that was true here in Sioux City).
11. Because of the above, Canada negotiated with China for crude oil.

12. This also took us from being energy-independent to dependence on foreign oil. (Maybe Alexandria Ocasio-Cortez and her friends would like to go to Texas and see what prosperity the Green New Deal will bring for us by switching from oil to wind energy.)
13. Biden supported the teacher's union refusing to teach.
14. Biden wanted us to double-mask (*Washington Post*) because we might not get back to normal until 2022 (CNN).
15. Iran likely backed the deadly rocket attack on US-led base, and Biden believed these people were reliable and wanted to return to normal relations with Iran, ignoring Trump's prize-winning peace efforts in that region.
16. Biden, with an executive order, destroyed any hope for female athletes to be equally competitive in their chosen sport events because they must compete with physically stronger males. (I hope you girls no longer have dreams of winning any female marathons.)
17. Biden committed $4 million of our tax money to help other countries with COVID-19 before Americans got the vaccine.
18. Biden refused to supply vaccine to border control and ICE officers.
19. Biden said during his campaign that anybody who ruled by executive order was a "dictator," yet he issued almost double the number of executive orders as Trump.
20. If the first thirty days is indicative of Biden's administration, this nation will be transformed into a socialist country faster than we could dream possible.

As of this writing, we have passed the third month of the Biden administration. I feel it is the responsibility of each citizen to evaluate our political leaders and the direction they are leading the nation.

According to *The Interpreter's Dictionary of the Bible*, recognizing the meaning of prophecy as history is defined as reflecting only the "divine concerns," as well as having "divine purpose" and "divine participation." If we consider the first three months of the Biden administration from a prophetic point of view, will we find divine concerns, divine purpose, and divine participation? Let's compare the divine perspectives of the Trump administration with the Biden administration. It would take volumes to deal with all issues but let's look at a few.

Just hours after accepting the presidency, Biden ended the building of the XL pipeline. Many argue that when President Trump overruled the prior administration's prevention of building the pipeline, he was doing a divine act because it allowed for safer means for petroleum to get from one area to another. With the built-in safety features, such as automatic shutdown if a slight decrease in pressure occurred, very little contamination would take place. The system may not be perfect, many argued, but it would eliminate hauling by trucks and transporting by rail, both of which is costly and more dangerous to human life and the environment.

The other side of this debate states that the pipeline goes right through the largest lake of fresh water in North America. The lake lies underground but is vulnerable to contamination from the surface. As I said, the pipeline has built-in security devices that would shut it down immediately. (At least, that's what I've been told.) No human project or creation is perfect, so the question becomes this: is the cancellation of this pipeline based on divine concern or based on fear? Does it enhance divine purpose to offer lower prices and, thus, savings for Americans, or does it offer large benefits for truck haulers and railroad companies? Does the pipeline offer divine participation by allowing us to have faith that the fears expressed will not develop as they predicted, and that God will bring us valued and improved services? Or are we to accept the idea that anything humans strive to create and work to achieve is total folly, corrupt, and not of value to anybody?

I've thought of President Biden's first press conference, and I think the most significant issue was the lack of truth. In his book *The Theft of America's Soul*, Phil Robertson titled one of his chapters "The Lie: Truth is relative. The Truth: There is absolute truth, and it comes from God." If you listened carefully to the questions and responses by the president, I'm not sure you would find absolute truth. The first thing we saw was President Biden looking at pictured listings of whom he should call first for a question, and then who was scheduled as number two, then number three, etc. With a certain camera angle, you could see numbers by the pictures. With that information, we must ask: Did these reporters truthfully give their questions before the press conference began? With almost every question, Biden looked at notes so that he could give what appeared to be a prepared authorized answer. Also, on several occasions, Biden made absolute false statements, primarily against his predecessor Donald Trump. I know that Donald Trump was not perfect in everything he said, but I cannot recall any direct, outright lie that he deliberately spoke—I'm not saying it did not happen; I'm saying I don't recall any. I say this because I have heard reporters claim a lie was stated, but if you listen carefully, you will know that the reporter failed to listen.

With all this, I must raise the question: was this meet-the-press meeting of divine concern? The answer to that would be a positive yes. God has always been concerned with what kings, dictators, and presidents tell their (God's) people. Then was this meeting to tell the American people the message of unity that Biden promised in his inaugural address? I don't see how anyone could say it was unifying. Was the overall result of the press conference seen as fulfilling the promise to unify the nation; did it fulfill divine purpose? I don't think it answered any real issues that were raised since Biden became president, nor did it fulfill any purpose that

God would ask of a leader. The truth is that no divine purpose was achieved was because when there are lies and misrepresentation, as all indications showed, and everything was preplanned, how can there be participation from God, who proclaims righteousness and justice, truth and honor, peace, and joy? After listening to that hour-long question-and-answer press conference, I was more confused, more upset, and a lot more distrustful of Biden, of the government, and of the media.

I was more distrustful of Biden for the obvious reason—he was elected to bring transparency and truth. I believe Biden is more of a puppet whose strings are being pulled by the rich and the powerful from outside the government. I was more distrustful of government because I knew that the Democrats all supported Biden, and so did all his appointees. Perhaps they kept their minds closed to truths about him being a puppet. I was more distrustful of the media because after watching press meetings with Donald Trump and how the reporters blasted him with questions and accusations, and then reported partial responses and gave false opinions and ideas, there's little to trust about what happened at Biden's first press conference and the media.

I wish there were better things to say. I hate saying such negative things, especially about our president and other leaders, but the truth is, they sought the positions they have, and they are responsible. I often think about the statement Jesus made after a discussion with a rich young person, who was asking how he could enter the kingdom of heaven. After the gentleman had left. Jesus said that it is easier for a camel to go through the eye of a needle than for a rich man to get into heaven. It seems all other sins are less severe than being rich. I believe this includes positions of power.

Perhaps it has something to do with the statement referred to earlier when Jesus was departing for the last time. If we forgive the sins of others, those sins will be forgiven; if we cannot forgive their sins, they will not be forgiven. This, of course, is speculation, but it seems to me that no one becomes wealthy or powerful without hurting or even totally destroying someone else, nor do they achieve what they seek without lying, stealing, and doing whatever they need to do against thousands or even millions. Can you imagine the number of people who will be required to forgive representatives, senators, governors, presidents, kings, and CEOs before they will receive the forgiveness needed so that God can forgive? As I said, this is speculation because we know that with God, all things are possible. After thinking about these things, I feel that the following scripture somehow sums up what this amounts to:

> Then Jesus said to them, "You are such foolish people. You find it so hard to believe all that the prophets wrote in the scriptures. Wasn't it clearly predicted by the prophets that the Messiah would have to suffer all these things before entering his time of glory?" (Luke 24:23–26)

How many times did God tell His children—and especially their leaders—that if they failed to follow His commands that they would be punished and/or destroyed? How many of the nations that God created after AD. 70 did He destroy and then create another nation westward? How many early settlers moved west when they believed their communities had become too secular?

We do not have prophets shouting warnings, nor do we have God telling us to correct our actions or we will be destroyed— or do we? Why do we find it so hard to believe what scripture and history have told us, as well as those who talk to us about the Constitution and the Bill of Rights—that breaking our laws and morale laws, including the laws given to us in scripture, will have dire consequences?

After taking a break from writing for several hours, I later opened my Bible and read the following:

> But no, my people wouldn't listen. Israel did not want me around. So, I let them follow their blind and stubborn way, living according to their own desires. But oh, that my people would listen to me! Oh, that Israel would follow me, walking in my paths! How quickly I would then subdue their enemies! (Psalm 81:11–14)

"How quickly I would subdue their enemies!" How much clearer of a message do we need? Just before I started reading, I was checking news commentaries, and I heard that we need to reform our universities and colleges. The commentators mentioned that the Democrats had opened the border to allow illegal immigrants to enter and were trying to make it a national policy that anyone who got any form of government monies would automatically be a registered voter, thus allowing millions of the illegal individuals the right to vote. They also pointed out that President Biden stopped the 1776 report, which was intended to bring back to our schools the traditional history of the United States. There was also a discussion on how the Democrats have falsely stated that whites are responsible for the greatest number of black and Hispanic deaths, but according to FBI statistics, it is blacks that kill more blacks and Hispanics. There were also reports on how damaging these COVID government handouts are, although they are really tempting. Oh, that my people would listen and follow God, walking in his paths.

Chapter 9

You might think that all these things—all the unjust actions brought upon us—are only because of government policies, but they are also because of social and commercial media. The truth also must include the sins by the American citizens. When I hear reports that millions of abortions are performed every year, I know the Lord our God is keenly aware of these things. Americans seek the many gifts the Lord has made available for us, and so we purchase items we do not need with credit cards, thus making us dependent upon Mastercard rather than God, who knows our needs. In our desire for the better life, we allow ourselves to be persuaded into abandoning our peace and joy of Christ. After reading Habakkuk 1:14–17 "Are we but fish to be caught and killed? … Will you let them get away with this forever?"—we must admit that in our country, the sins of our leaders are, in part, created by our own sins and our actions. Our leaders, however, are responsible for giving us the ability and allowing us to make our own choices.

> Save me, O God, for the floodwaters are upon my neck … Those who hate me without cause are more numerous than the hairs on my head. (Psalm 69)

Every day, it seems, we are losing the rights given to us in the Bill of Rights—"for the floodwaters are upon my neck." A leader for women's rights pointed out that with all the distinctions of the sexes, the researchers at the CDC (Centers for Disease Control and Prevention) who are investigating the effects that drugs have on women and men will no longer be done because there officially are no female and male genders. The two genders do have physical differences, so drugs for one gender may negatively affect the other; medicine a woman takes just might kill her husband. In addition, those who hate God are taking COVID-19 relief money and using it to bail out sanctuary cities and states. Criminals who have committed major crimes are being let out of prison without doing the complete time allocated by the justice system from which they were sentenced, thus prohibiting justice for the innocent.

> One day the Pharisees asked Jesus, "When will the Kingdom of God come?" Jesus replied, "The Kingdom of God isn't ushered in with visible signs. You won't be able to say, 'Here it is' or 'It's over there! For the Kingdom of God is among you." (Luke 17:20)

For the Kingdom of God is among you. What could Jesus possibly be saying? First, Christians are very aware that as we live our daily lives, God is with us. For example, Christians are living among people who are living in fear of the coronavirus. We listen to the science and their priests and often follow their guidelines of wearing masks and keeping social distance, but we do this as Paul recommended to his fellow church members—not to eat meat offered as a sacrifice to idols because it might offend someone. Even though we do not fear the virus, we wear masks, so we don't offend those living in fear. Many have shared with me their anger that we must wear masks, rather than publicly profess our faith that God is protecting us.

There are no "visible signs" of the kingdom of God, yet we are confronted with signs of government leaders and with corporate and businesspeople who turn many aspects of our security and financial independence over to our number-one adversary, the Chinese Communist Party. These, too, are actions allowed by God. Remember Habakkuk? "O Lord our Rock, you have decreed the rise of these Babylonians to punish and correct us for our terrible sins" (1:12). And in Luke, Jesus replied, "Just as the gathering of vultures shows there is a carcass nearby, so these signs indicate that the end is near" (Luke 17:37).

You might be wondering how this relates to the United States being the John the Baptist of nations. As we learned earlier, John's purpose was not to create a new religion but to prepare the way for Christ. Yet his message was new. He baptized with water to wash away sins, but Christ's message was to be baptized with the Holy Spirit and receive eternal life. The difference between prior Christian nations and the acts of punishment and corrections against them is that we come to the idea that God could move west to create a new nation. Today we have no "west" to which we can escape, and God has no new territory where He can create a new nation. While people are destroying the Judeo-Christian world that God has created, He has no place to rebuild. Prior acts corrected the errors of those nations, but to destroy this nation would be to enter into the years of the Antichrist.

If the United States is the final nation, as a forerunner to the thousand-year reign of Christ, we then represent the end of something that has been sought by millions of people around the world. We also represent the beginning of something much greater. F. F. Bruce commented on Paul's conversion experience on the road to Damascus. Paul recognized the meaning of the cross.

> And then, without warning, the Crucified One
> appeared to him in a form too compelling to admit

of any doubts and identified himself to Paul as 'Jesus of Nazareth, whom you are persecuting' (Acts 22:8; also 26:15). The disciples had been right after all: the 'hanged man' had indeed risen from the dead and must consequently be acknowledged as Lord and Messiah. The pronouncement of the divine curse on the hanged man still stood in the Law; it must therefore be accepted that the Messiah had incurred this curse, but now this paradox had to be considered and explained. Sooner rather than later, Paul saw the solution of the problem in the argument which he expounds in Gal 3:10-14 where he says that Christ, in accepting death by crucifixion, voluntarily submitted to the divine curse and thus released his people from the curse which the Law pronounces on all who break it (Deut. 27;26) by 'becoming a curse' on their behalf. (241)

First, then, we must acknowledge that the "old" curse brought death to us. Then, the "new" death brought us life. The old for us, as a nation, is the creation and fulfillment of the Judeo-Christian society. The new will be the end of our nation and the coming of Christ's kingdom for one thousand years. The new for Paul was to preach the great news of salvation. The new for humankind, looking at it from a bird's-eye view of history, was the creation of the church, then the creation of the Christian nations, followed by the Judeo-Christian nation, the United States.

I believe with all my heart that the next phase of history has begun; it began with the creation of Israel. If the miracles of scripture tell us anything, it's that we must recognize that the persecution of the Jews by Hitler, followed by the creation of Israel, is something we cannot ignore as being part of God's overall plan. Nor can we imagine or comprehend the role that Israel will have in the future. This much I do believe: God will bless anyone who blesses what God has created—the chosen people of Abraham, the Christians and the church, the United States, and now, the new Israel. God will curse anyone who curses the chosen people of Abraham, the Christians and the church, the United States, and the new Israel.

Will the United States have to die, like John the Baptist? According to what I was told almost sixty years ago, the answer is yes. If that is so, we must remember what happened after John was killed—Christ's kingdom of grace became a reality.

Chapter 10

As a citizen, I felt obligated to listen to President Biden's first national address concerning the first anniversary of the COVID-19 virus and the national shutdown. I listened with the understanding that before I die, I'll "witness the downfall of the United States." That night, I read first from Psalms and then from Luke, followed by Zephaniah.

> Endow the king with your justice, O God, the royal son with your righteousness. He will judge your people in righteousness, your afflicted ones with justice. (Psalm 72:1–2)

To me, there is no better expression of what we should expect from our president and no better opportunity for us to hear such expressions. Granted, there was some expression of understanding and compassion for the millions who have suffered because of the virus. But as I listened, I did not hear any kind of righteous talk from his actions. Righteous talk would have been to acknowledge the work done by his predecessor because regardless of political opposition, the prior acts brought medical and psychological healing to America.

In Luke 18:31–34, Jesus again predicts his death:

> He will be handed over to the Romans to be mocked, treated shamefully and spit upon. They

will whip him and kill him, and on the third day
will rise again. (Luke 18:32–33)

Although I heard words of compassion in Biden's first national
address, the overriding message, as I listened, was a mockery
of not only our constitutional rights but also a shameful lack of
acknowledgment for what was done prior to his becoming president.
Many men and women were committed to developing medicines
and vaccines, and his predecessor changed the process so that
millions of people, including President Biden, could be vaccinated,
but this was not acknowledged. By deliberately omitting such
remarks, President Biden not only unjustly treated former president
Trump but—more importantly—he unjustly treated those who
did the work.

I then turned to Zephaniah:

> And I [God] will destroy those who used to worship
> me but now no longer do. They no longer ask for
> the Lord's guidance or seek my blessings … That
> terrible day of the Lord is near. Swiftly it comes—a
> day when strong men will cry bitterly … Gather
> together and pray, you shameless nation. Gather
> while there is still time … Gaza, Askelon, Ashdod,
> Ekron—these Philistine cities, too, will be rooted
> out and left in desolation. And how terrible it will
> be for you Philistines who live along the coast and
> in the land of Canaan, for this judgment is against
> you, too! (Zephaniah 1:6, 14; 2:1–2)

It's important to note that I did not search for these words, but
they were there to read. How could anyone see what took place in
New York, Washington, DC, California, Portland, or Minneapolis
throughout the summer of 2020 and not question what the future

will be like? At no point during the president's speech concerning the events of the past year did I hear condemnation of how and where the virus originated. I didn't hear an explanation as to why, in primarily Democratic cities, with their policies to shut down, so many have suffered, compared to the areas where there were no shutdown policies. I heard that if we did not follow the guidelines of the gods of science and the words of their priests, we would be forced to rescind the rights once again, and we, the citizens, would *not* be free to gather together on the Fourth of July.

Let me put this into perspective. I think of 1960, when God showed me that He created this nation, and then of 1962, when He told me I would witness the destruction of the nation I love. Why do I have such feelings about our nation? It begins with the idea of *good*.

> For the idea of the good did not create life, it has no interest in life. It is an alien force ... [but] It is He [God] who unites what is (good) with what ought to be ... His will is the source of that which is (good) and the basis of that which ought to be. (Brunner, 114)

Therefore, if we do not seek good, which is the *He*, and we do not do that which "*ought to be*," then we are not agents of the will of God. If we are not agents of the will of God, then we are agents of Satan. This means that God is the one who created this nation (the good), and if we do not continue to do that which is doing the good, which God created (that which ought to be), then that which was created good will no longer exist.

The good that God offers is brought to us as love. The true definition of love comes from Jesus Christ.

> That which *we* call "love" is always a conditional self-giving, whether it be the love of a mother, or the love of country, or the love of an idea. It is always a love which is limited to some secret demand for compensation, or by some relic of exclusiveness. (Brunner, 115)

This means that people, even presidents, can say they love us, but is that love based on what they "demand for compensation"? The gods and priests of science have dictated that we must follow their rules and regulations—we must wear masks; we must follow social distancing; we must keep our businesses closed; we must not gather in large groups. And we must not realize where all these directives come from. "Certain friends and business agreements" come from those whose true purpose is to destroy us and control the world. (Have you heard of Hunter Biden and his and his father's cooperation with the Chinese Communist Party? The idea is that Hunter traveled to China on Air Force 2 with his dad, Joe, and returned with millions of dollars in contracts.) So those whose true purpose is to destroy us—the CCP, now associated with Hunter and Joe Biden—have their own "demand for compensation." I can hear my critics crying, preparing to mock me, spit on me, whip me. Christ said there would be days like this.

> Therefore, the demands of love can never be separated from the claims of God Himself. (Brunner 117)

> The humanitarian ethic seem possible, owing to the historical fact that the love which is based upon the Christian revelation can exist for a time as an idea even when severed. (Brunner, 600)

Therefore, people can say they love, even though their love is "severed" from Christ because they have self-giving motives. God's love, in the here and now, is not necessarily the idea of love that we find in scripture. Reading about love does not always mean it is the love from God.

> Therefore, we can never know beforehand what God will require. God's command can only be perceived at the actual moment of hearing it. ... Therefore, it is impossible for us to know it beforehand; to wish to know it beforehand—legalism—is an infringement of the divine honor. The fact that the holiness of God must be remembered when we dwell on his love means that we cannot have his love at our disposal, that it cannot ever be perceived as a universal principle. (Brunner, 117–8)

Brunner is saying that God's command is understood only after He has revealed to us what His intentions are. Considering the history of our nation, our men and women (granted, the women were in the background) studied and witnessed other forms of government, and after many debates and meetings with various individuals who expressed ideas in writing, our forefathers created a nation that other nations either copied or totally rejected. Just like the creation of the Israel of old, so many mistakes were made, and many developments had to be corrected and fought for. The holiness of God, as He created the new nation, cannot be "perceived as a universal principle" but must be adhered to as the foundation for advancement. Thus, to replace the foundation with complete destruction and to build a new foundation based on socialism is to sever God's revelation concerning our Judeo-Christian nation; it would be like severing Christ and the crucifixion and the

Resurrection from God's love for us as individuals. Again, turning to Emil Brunner:

> It is, of course, true that we know God's love in his Word which is also a *deed, i*n the Holy Scriptures. But this Word which has actually occurred can only be perceived as HIS word which is now living and active ... through the Holy Spirit. This applies not only to the knowledge for that which God *wills* for us, but also for that which he desires to have *from* us ... Real faith always means obedience to God. (118)

For President Biden to profess his profound Roman Catholic faith but then to write executive orders (which he admitted would be the acts of a dictator) is to undermine the *deed* that God created through the Holy Spirit and the foundation for this nation of using the legislative process, rather than executive order. Thus, in replacing the foundation with socialism (totalitarianism), Biden then took away that which God *wills* to us—the legislative process—but he also took from us that which God desires *from* us, which is the ability to vote and to hold our legislators responsible for their acts.

We must consider one more characteristic of this question of ethics: is the good that we do founded in our self-interest, or is it founded in God?

> To do the Good for the sake of the Good is only the pale reflection of the genuine Good; to do the Good for the sake of God means to do the Good not because my moral dignity requires it, but because it is what God commanded. (Brunner, 121)

For politicians and/or CEOs to seek good things themselves or their constituents or stockholders is good, but the question is this: Is the good they seek founded in God or in self-interest? If what the politician seeks comes from the foundation created by God—as laid before us in the Constitution and the Bill of Rights—then historically good acts are based on righteousness and justice for all and not just a few contributors; and then—and only then—those acts are founded in God. For the CEOs, if the good they seek is fairness to the American customer and not just to the stockholders, then they are founded in God.

After giving some regulations in his first letter to the Thessalonians, Paul wrote:

> Anyone who refuses to live by these rules is not disobeying human rules but is rejecting God, who gives his Holy Spirit to you. (Thessalonians 4:8)

Biden, by not acknowledging the accomplishments of a former president—thus, not acknowledging history—is not "disobeying human rules but is rejecting God." In Paul's letter to the Romans, he wrote, "So God let them go ahead and do whatever shameful things their hearts desired" (Romans 1:24). As such, God let Biden go ahead and tell us what he wanted us to hear.

In Phil Robertson's book *The Theft of America's Soul*, he referred to Revelations 21:8:

> But cowards who turn away from me, and unbelievers, and the corrupt, and murderers, and the immoral, and those who practice witchcraft, and idol worshipers, and all liars--their doom is in the lake that burns fire and sulfur. This is the second death.

The sins of our leaders are more than personal. Biden's speech was not his bedside talk with God; it affected all of us because he was talking to all of us. It is true that our leaders will be confronted with their sins and must seek personal forgiveness. The question is this: do we need to accept their sins that affect us? The answer is no.

I like the story John told when Christ was departing from His followers during His last appearance. He told them, "If you forgive anyone's sins, they are forgiven, if you refuse to forgive them, they are unforgiven" (John 20:23). I have thought about the awesome responsibility that we, as Christians, are given with this statement, but I also think about what might have happened before Jesus's final appearance. I picture Jesus in heaven with God, who hosted a heavenly dinner for His Son because of what Jesus did for the children of God. I picture Moses giving a speech, celebrating Jesus as the ultimate priest, leading the people to eternal life. I picture David congratulating Jesus as King, and Elijah talking about Christ's accomplishments as a prophet. I then see, after the celebration, God walking with His arm around Jesus, telling Him how proud He is of what Christ did but then saying something to the effect that Christ did such a great job of showing love that God was afraid people might lose the reality that God is a God of righteousness and justice, and without these, there is no love.

So it is that our leaders must be honest and speak the truth, even if it is not to our liking. I believe that was what President Trump did. I believe he was like a father telling his kids why they should not play with fire or why they needed to have a curfew. Our leaders need to be strong, not just in words but in actions, such as securing our borders and eliminating orders that hinder progress and health. Our leaders must not seek to destroy our fundamental rights, which are given to us by God, not by governments. The people must vote for these leaders; they should not be chosen by the deep state to be part of a committee creating laws.

If politicians do not do their best and fight to keep the promises they made during their campaigns, then they are liars and self-seeking, not representatives of our interests. We have no responsibility to keep them in office; in fact, we have an obligation to vote them out of office. Christ came for the last time and told us that if we forgive, the sins are forgiven; if not, the sins are not forgiven. We can forgive, but we do not need to support.

Chapter 11

It is important that we understand that we, as individuals, do not have the authority to decide another person's relationship with God. It is as the psalmist wrote:

> If I had really spoken this way, I would have been a traitor to your people. So I tried to understand why the wicked prosper. But what a difficult task it is! Then one day I went into your sanctuary, O God, and I thought about the destiny of the wicked. Truly, you put them on a slippery path and send them sliding over the cliff to destruction. (Psalm 73:15–18)

It is not for us to know why God allows the wicked to destroy nations. It baffles me why the rich, who have gained their wealth in this country, contribute to those who work to destroy that which gave them the opportunity to make their wealth. The psalm of Asaph offers these words:

> For no one on earth—from east to west, or even from the wilderness—can raise another person up. It is God alone who judges; he decides who will rise and who will fall. (Psalm 75:6–7)

God will keep His promises to the thousands who will be able to go to the Father. God will disregard the generations who will be outside crying, "Why not me, Lord?" We do not have the power or the authority to save this nation, just as John the Baptist had no power to get out of prison or to save his life. I believe if we faithfully act by voting for those who confess their faith in God, He will allow us to continue. "If you forgive anyone's sins, they will be forgiven."

Over the years, I have talked with several individuals (professionals and friends) about forgiveness. As I expected, their collective response was that the Lord tells us to forgive, and science (psychologists) tells us that to forgive is best for us; it gives us peace of mind.

I cannot recall one person who caused me not to forgive, but I have a nagging feeling that somewhere, someone has difficulty in trying to forgive. There are times when we confess that we forgive someone with our minds and with our lips, but the truth is that deep in our hearts and souls, that forgiveness does not feel complete. It is not that this causes us distress or that we ponder the issue day and night. It's just *there*. I believe this was why Jesus made it clear that there might be times when the hurt and the pain someone caused is so profound that forgiveness just doesn't come.

God knows our feelings. Read the account of Jesus after He came from the mountain after His experience with Moses and Elijah, and consider the emotions he must have felt, only to be immediately confronted with the situation with His disciples. They had been struggling to heal the boy with demons, but their efforts had failed. Jesus, in a complete turnaround from moments earlier, said, "You stubborn, faithless people, how long must I be with you and put up with you?" (Luke 9:41).

Another example was Christ's prayer while in the garden of Gethsemane:

> And now I am coming to you. I have told them [his disciples] many things while I was with them so they would be filled with my joy. I have given them your word. And the world hates them because they do not belong to the world, just as I do not. I'm not asking you to take them out of the world, but to keep them safe from the evil one. (John 17:13–15)

I believe we have witnessed profoundly deep feelings that Christ carried in His soul, which illustrates that we, too, can carry profound feelings, and they won't alter who we are or how we live with others. Thinking that we cannot find peace or joy until we forgive is an idea that Satan wants us to believe. But as Christians, although forgiveness ranks high in finding peace, we ultimately find peace with God's love. For Christians, love and forgiveness includes righteousness and justice. True righteousness and justice come from God, and we Christians can have peace and joy because we are in God's love, blameless from not being able to forgive. I've found out, however, that time does heal, and I do believe that, as time passes, Christ, our brother, does give us the ability to forgive.

You're probably wondering how this corresponds to the issue of the United States being the John the Baptist of nations. I've spent some time on this matter because I feel Christ's affection, expressed in the prayer quoted above, for His disciples. "I have given them your word. ... I'm not asking you to take them out of the world, but to keep them safe from the evil one." This is what I feel that God has given to me. He has allowed me to live in this country at this time in its history, rather than to join my sister, so that I could tell America why God created this nation.

Jesus did not condemn the world. He did recognize the power of the "evil one," yet He prayed for the welfare and the blessings for His disciples. He concludes his prayer with the following:

O righteous Father, the world doesn't know you,
but I do; and these disciples know you sent me.
And I have revealed you to them and will keep on
revealing you. I will do this so that your love for
me may be in them and I in them. (John 17:25–26)

The world doesn't know God, but Christ does reveal God to us, and it is up to us to listen. I believe Christ has revealed to me—and to Donald J. Trump and to his followers and to all Americans who recognize the dangers in the fatal policies and actions of those now leading this country—that they are bringing us to the very edge of the cliff, to a fatal time. The current administration and the deep state, the nonelected authorities controlling our government, have already created policies that will destroy that for which thousands of men died to free us from England, who died to free us from the Nazis, and who have since given their lives to keep us free. The destructive acts also include the now-distorted news media, which reveals their true selves by reporting only what they want the American people to know. They report lies expressed by politicians and nonelected officials, lies fabricated by the media itself by distorting the truth, and lies of omission, by not telling the complete story.

Jesus, however, does reveal God to us. How does He do this as a nation? He reveals to us the history, the rights given to us by the Constitution, and the freedom expressed in the statement of independence and in our division of powers, both in the branches of federal government and by separating the state powers from the federal government. How do we fight to keep our Judeo-Christian society? I am fighting by writing this; you are fighting by reading this. We are fighting by praying and by voting for those who confess their faith in God and by getting involved, primarily in local affairs, and by writing or calling our representatives.

> Therefore the commandments of the Bible ... are absolutely necessary. The Apostles themselves experienced this; that is why they used to "exhort" their converts; that is why they ordered certain things to be done which seem to us quite obvious—just because—unfortunately—they were not obvious at all. ... From the law of love [the New Testament] the believer can know himself deduce law, since he "applied" it to particular cases. (Brunner, 149)

This is why we need the foundation—the Declaration of Independence, the Constitution, and the Bill of Rights—so love can deduce what needs to be applied to each executive order, each policy declared by our president, and each bill introduced by the House of Representatives and the Senate—and let's not forget the decisions made by our courts. Therefore, what we expect from our elected leaders—presidents, governors, mayors, representations in all levels of government—should be that they seek "the will of the loving Father, who wills nothing so much as to keep us within His love and His work," so that "who in faith is united with God and with his neighbor, that he may really act in harmony with love, and may not make a mistake" (Brunner, 150). With this, then, the "law exercises us at the same time in discipline, humility, and joyful childlike obedience" (Brunner, 151).

Discipline is the willingness to follow the Constitution. Humility is the willingness to go against those who work to undermine our foundation. Childlike obedience is the willingness to joyfully accept that what others before us did was right. I must confess, for the sake of our nation, that I see and feel hate from those who are not willing to admit the many things our forefathers, and now, Donald J. Trump and his army of like-minded individuals, have done. Their acts, when allowed to advance to their desired goals, were good for our nation.

As I was reading the other day, I found this:

> O my people, listen to my teaching, Open your ears to what I am saying, for I will speak to you in parable. I will teach you hidden lessons from our past stories we have heard and know, stories our ancestors handed down to us. We will not hide these truths from our children but will tell the next generation about the glorious deed of the Lord. We will tell of his power and the mighty miracles he did. (Psalm 78:1–4)

Let's look closer at what this says to us, as American citizens. "Listen." We need to be willing to listen to the history of our nation. We need to hear the voices of those from the past and those from other countries and understand why they seek to come here. We need to hear the voices of our ancestors, specifically from Old Testament stories of governing and messages from the prophets. My people will be told the truth so our children will know the glorious deeds that the Lord has done for us, so His power and mighty miracles will be known by the next generation.

We cannot allow the 1619 Project to infiltrate our schools; our children must hear the true history. The earlier history has some merit. Although I have not read the project's message, I'm sure there is some element of fact that can help us understand the human sin in history, but our children must learn what God has created so that they can distinguish what the lies and the evil Antifa, Black Lives Matter, and the Left political agenda truly is. They must understand what the socialistic, communistic, anti-Semitic hate for religion and religious freedom truly is and how it destroys what we have.

After reading the Psalm 78, I received inspiration from Luke:

> But as they came closer to Jerusalem and Jesus saw
> the city ahead, he began to cry. "I wish that even
> today you could find the way of peace." (Luke 28:1)

I cannot express how much these words hurt my soul because I believe Jesus cries with every untruthful newscast. It is unbelievable what is happening. I heard that we can no longer say "Happy Thanksgiving"; we must say "Happy People Day." Recently, a Chinese representative met with a US representative. This is, in part, what the Chinese representative said concerning the United States: Many people within the United States actually have little comfort in the US democracy, and they have various views regarding the US government. "We do not believe in invading, in the use of force, or to topple other regimes to various means, or to massacre the people of other countries because all of those would cause turmoil and instability in this world. It is important for the United States to change its own image and to stop advancing its own democracy in the rest of the world."

This view shows utter contempt for this country. Of course, this should be expected from a country that watches its citizens via nationwide cameras. They instantly know when someone climbs aboard a bus to go where they are not allowed to go. They place individuals into reeducation camps if they do not adhere to the Chinese Communist Party policies. He said they don't invade, use force, or massacre other countries, but what happened in Hong Kong? Keep your eye on Taiwan!

The real problem with the meeting was the response by Secretary of State Blinken and his lack of candor. His response was, "What I have to tell you is that what I am hearing is very different from what you described. What I am hearing is that there is deep satisfaction that America is back." It was what he did not say that represents our government's lack of dealing with truly meaningful talks with our enemy. China has lied for the past year about the COVID-19 virus, and Blinken refused to bring up the topic for discussion.

Under the Biden administration, we are forbidden to refer to the virus as the "Chinese virus" because it offends his friends and money relations with Chinese business associates. (I'm sorry! Joe Biden does *not* have business dealings with China; only his son does, but Joe gets, I believe, 10 percent. But Joe doesn't have ties with China.) If you believe that, I have an oceanside property in Arizona I'll sell you. The prophets in the Old Testaments constantly had to tell their kings how angry God would get when they ignored the welfare of their citizens for personal gains. "I wish even today that you could find the way to peace"

I recently watched the television miniseries *A.D.: The Bible Continues*. In one particular scene, just after the crucifixion, a group of people are talking:

"Day by day, more and more people were being seduced by the Nazarene's simplistic homilies. He had to be exposed."

"My husband took a decision any high priest would've taken."

"It was the needless death of a harmless soul."

"Harmless? He threatened everything we represent, and these people believed it. The life of one man is nothing, Joseph, for the sake of God's nation."

"Joseph and his lofty morals, floating above the daily game of public affairs. Ah, his words come cheap. Without actions to test them, his opinions are fruitless."

As I listened to these words, my mind told me that this conversation could easily be taking place in the halls of our federal buildings. I could hear the Right saying that day by day, more and more people are being seduced by ideas, and we have to expose them for what they are. Then the Left would say that they have to make some decisions that can be described as harmless and represent them as ideas that the Constitution was intended to represent.(For example, the passing of the COVID relief bill or the HR 1 bill are minor factors in the big scheme of government. The Left will spread their moral ideas, but their words come cheap, and without actions on their part, their words are fruitless.) The Right will fire back that they need to expose these "harmless" ideas and bills before they become law and destroy the very foundation of what the authors of our Constitution intended. For the sake of God's nation, we must act. We must act now and with complete determination.

In both illustrations, each side had understandable viewpoints. In the miniseries, the high priest made his decision based on false statements that were advocated by people who sought results that reflected their ideas of what was right. Finally, the high priest's decision was made, based on incomplete understanding of about whom he was speaking. The result of the actions was the Resurrection; in other words, it was exactly what God planned.

In my scenario, the Left is seeking power by false representation, whereas the Right is seeking the continuation of the nation God created. I believe this all ties in with Emil Brunner's description of the nature of human conscience. He pointed out that our consciences are not as we normally think; that is, we think that we have the ability to have the good thoughts our consciences express to us. Brunner argues that humankind cannot create good thoughts because of our state of sin, and the real agent of good thoughts is God.

> Faith awakens when man see himself, not in the
> light of conscience, but in the new light thrown
> upon his nature by the gracious word of God, in

ChristJesus. ... For before the Good can be done,
the agent [conscience] must be good. But the only
Doer of Good deeds is God. Man, therefore, can
only do good deeds in so far as God does them in
him, in so far as our action is obedience to the will
of God, wrought in us by God himself. (158, 162)

Therefore, if man does not do good deeds, does that mean that
God is not "in him"? Let me put it like this: If the representatives
and/or citizens don't do good deeds, does that mean that God is no
longer in the nation? After sixty days into the Biden administration,
I believe God is opening the door to walk out; that is, God is
preparing to walk away from the United States. If so, the comment
I heard back in high school—that I would see the downfall of this
nation before I die—will be a true statement. Then, my days will
be numbered.

I remember the story that Daniel wrote. He had been seeking a
message from God. Finally, an angel appeared and said:

Don't be afraid, Daniel. Since the first day you
began to pray ... your request has been heard
in heaven ... I have come in answer ... But for
twenty-one days the spirit prince of the kingdom
of Persia blocked my way. Then Michael, one of
the archangels, came to help me, and I left him
there with the spirit prince of the kingdom of
Persia. Now I am here ... Soon I must return
to fight against the spirit prince of the kingdom
Persia, and then against the spirit prince of the
kingdom of Greece ... (There is no one to help me
against these spirit princes except Michael, your
spirit prince. I have been standing beside Michael
as his support and defense since the first year of

the reign of Darius the Mede.) (Daniel 10:12–14,
20–21; 11:1)

God told us in this vision that there are forces at war with
each other. Darius the Mede was the new ruler of Babylon who
let the people of God return to Jerusalem and then supported the
rebuilding of the temple. It was the angel, along with the archangel
Michael, who guarded Darius and allowed him to free the Jews.

I believe we have angels guarding this nation, but the question
is this: how long will God allow them to keep their guard?

Chapter 12

As I continued my nightly readings, I came to this: as Jesus's followers were gathered together after his Resurrection, "Jesus himself was suddenly standing there among them. He said, 'Peace be with you.' But the whole group was terribly frightened ... 'Why are you frightened? Why do you doubt who I am?'" (Luke 24:36–37). Doesn't this truly represent us? I don't know what it is about us that we seem to stiffen up when the name of Jesus is brought into our conversations. We seem to shy away from introducing Jesus into our business meetings.

I once read an example of how we can build confidence in bringing Jesus into our relationships with other people. Dr. Norman Vincent Peale wrote that his family would set a place at their dinner table and would picture Jesus sitting with them.

These thoughts lead us to the concept of how we should act to show what our relationship with Christ can bring to others—what is it that we truly feel. The task of citizenship is an understanding of right behavior. So, then, the question is: what is the right behavior? Who determines what the right behavior really is? Terms used to describe the right behavior lead to the idea of perfect equality, but for the "Christian, the idea of love breaks through and removes 'the basic idea of equality'" (Brunner, 182). So, the idea of righteousness, described as perfect equality, is also described as *equity*—a term we have heard a great deal since the advancement of the social Left. Equity, when understood, "makes it very plain that true justice cannot be conceived in legal terms … There is no 'static' equity, only an equity which *can be discovered at the moment of action"* (Brunner, 180).

So, then, the definition of *good* is determined at the moment. Therefore, what is good today may not be good tomorrow, depending on the situation and who is defining what is good. It is true that Christian's ought to have this kind of love—that is, love that is needed at that moment—but only in a limited sense. This basic idea of equity, as described by Aristotle, was carried over by theologians in their understanding of ethics. But the Reformer rejected this understanding, which the Pilgrims brought to the New World. What the Pilgrims rejected was the idea that the good has to be discovered, and the power of the discovery is recognized not at that moment but by God. This, they realized, was just the beginning, for they knew that the one who defines what is good is also the one who has the power to judge what must take place and what must happen, either for the good or for the bad. They then turned to the best source of what they recognized as what was good and what was evil, and that was from the scriptures (from God).

I have thought of a couple of examples that highlight the idea of equity and why this idea should or should not be used in the name of Christian ethics. As I said, the early theologians accepted the Aristotle's understanding of equity, and because she is a professed Catholic, my first example is Alexandria Ocasio-Cortez and her comrades. They must not have been updated in their understanding of the Catholic faith. She and they have come out strongly with dramatized ideas about climate change and the Green New Deal. She has described what will happen and what we must do to prevent the destruction of our land and our society, based on what is happening at this moment.

President Biden, in his first press briefing, stated that we need to raise the height of all our roads by three feet because of the devastation from climate change. Apparently, Ocasio-Cortez has discovered at the moment the good that needs to be done: convert all window-laden buildings to windowless buildings and eliminate all gas-powered automobiles and trucks, airplanes, and coal-powered plants. Yet they can buy million-dollar mansions on the seashore (as did former president Obama).

Here's another example of equity governing practices: In America today, in order to purchase a gun, an individual must answer questions on a federal questionnaire; to lie on the form results in heavy fines and/or imprisonment. One of the questions asks if the individual has a history of using illegal drugs. Of course, the president was not the one who created this "good" and safety-motivated question, but he, as chief executive for law enforcement, has the responsibility to compel enforcement of the law. It has been discovered that Hunter Biden, the son of the president, purchased a gun and lied on the form. It is also well known that Hunter was discharged from our military because he was caught using illegal drugs. As of this writing, under the guidelines of equity, Hunter has not been held accountable for this breach of conduct. So it is that equity makes it very plain that true justice cannot be conceived in legal terms.

I believe we need to consider another element of equity that is, in all reality, destroying this country. Donald J. Trump realized this issue and, working diligently with Senate Majority Leader Mitch McConnell, managed to correct this devastating governing flaw. I am referring to the appointment of many liberal judges—men and women who used their power not merely to judge if a law followed the principles of our Constitution but to alter it or, by judicial arguments and rulings, to create new laws. This procedure is strictly against the Constitution because laws are to be established by our legislative branch; that, is the House of Representatives and the Senate. These judges believed that after determining the good that was needed to eliminate a bad law, they also had the power to create a new law.

This is contrary to what our founding fathers established. They knew the ethical justice that was needed for a secure and just nation, and the best solution was to require the separation of powers so that no one person or party could determine what is right today but may not be right tomorrow. God had a guiding influence in the thoughts and debates that allowed our forefathers the ability to create this nation to prepare for the coming of Christ. Remember that we have run out of territory, and now we are destroying the John the Baptist of nations by destroying the fundamental principles created by our forefathers.

> But no, my people wouldn't listen. Israel did not want me around. So I let them follow their blind and stubborn way, living according to their own desires. (Psalm 81:11–12)

Equity has become such a major factor in our society today. I believe it is important to recognize that the practice is not limited to our leaders and judges. We, the citizens, must confront this problem of deciding what is good and then take the power to decide what we must do. I am thinking of the issue of abortion.

Let's first understand how the issue of equity applies to abortion. Remember that with equity, we have the power of discovery, and then we have the power to act according to what we believe is good. We start with the discovery of strong feelings, both the feelings of affection and the physical feelings resulting in sex. At this point, the circumstance doesn't matter—first date, engaged, married. The *good* at the moment must be evaluated to determine if the actions are for the good of tomorrow. As such, we can use the power to alter that which might result from the good of the moment.

The use of condoms would be the best act to prevent various

results for the future. There is no static in equity; we can follow our feelings or have the power to control those feelings. But then, we move on to the reality of pregnancy—the good of new life and the power of discovery to abort that life. The power is the ability to judge, considering our age, our family conditions, our living environment, our economic situation, and all the other factors. These questions to which we cannot know the answer. We cannot know what tomorrow will bring. There is only one thing that we do know, and that is that when we stand before God, we will be found wanting (Brunner, 185).

Therefore, the real question we have to ask is this: what does God tell us? What does our faith tell us? For some, it's a morality question. We think about all the issues in life that God provides for us, but all these situations are unknowable factors in the future. The one thing that God has made clear is that we shall not kill. Scripture also tells us in many places that God knew us even before conception.

I refer you to John's description of what happened just before Jesus was arrested. This is part of the prayer Jesus prayed:

> For you have given him (Jesus) authority over everyone in all the earth. He gives eternal life to each one you have given him ... And now, Father, bring me into the glory we shared before the world began. I have told these men about you. They were in the world but then you gave them to me. Actually, they were always yours, and you gave them to me; and they have kept your word. Now they know that everything I have is a gift from you, for I have passed on to them the words you gave me; and they accepted them and know that I came from you, and they believe you sent me. (John 17:2–6)

I'm going to go out on a very thin limb to express an idea that many will find difficult to accept; many may accuse me of heresy. But I believe we have been given a false conception. The church has somehow given us the idea that God, in His divine mercy, has granted all children, even those not yet born, heavenly joy. I truly wish this was true, but I cannot find it in scripture. I believe this idea is true for the children of believing parents only.

Remember God's three priorities for humankind: the individual, the family, and the nation. Also remember the statement that thousands will enter into the presence of God, but generations will be standing outside and crying, *Why not me?* I cannot ignore the truth of what happened in two specific incidents. The first is the story of Noah and the building of the ark. You'll recall that humankind had become so corrupt, so evil, that God questioned His own purpose in creating man and was on the verge of destroying everything. But then His council noticed Noah. It was God's council, probably Jesus, who pointed out Noah's righteousness. As a result, God told Noah to build the ark, which God Himself designed. The problem was that He designed a ship large enough for Noah and his family, as well as a male and female of each living species, but it wasn't large enough for all the infants and little children in the world. Their fate was destined to be with their parents.

Another example is the time when a few individuals, while in the wilderness, decided that the leadership that Moses was offering—and which was actually the plan that God had intended for the Israelites—was no longer acceptable to them. They believed that God had deserted them and so they created a situation we would classify as a civil war. When Moses heard about their plan, he called together the entire nation and offered them a choice. They could follow him, or they could go their own way and join those who led the rebellion. After the people made their decisions, God also made a decision. He opened up the earth:

And swallowed the men, along with their
household and the followers who were standing
with them and everything they owned. So they
went down alive into the grave, along with their
belongings. (Numbers 17:12–13)

The earth swallowed the men and their households, including
their wives and children. As much as I want, I cannot find these acts
of future generations altered. Jesus said to bring the little children
to Him, for of such is the kingdom of God. But this does not express
the idea that all children will be given to Him. The truth is we
parents, and church leaders must bring the children to Jesus. I do
not see the reality of the aforementioned stories being changed,
and as such, the idea that all aborted children will automatically
be escorted to heaven does not seem acceptable.

You may be wondering where the hope is. What can bring these
unborn souls to their rightful destination? Remember that a day
for the Lord is like a thousand years for humans, which means
that a moment in time for us and then to advance many years
later is just a few seconds for the Lord. An abortion today by an
unbelieving mother or father does mean the unborn child will be
denied entrance into heaven. Within seconds (for the Lord's time,
yet many years later for the mother or father), they find the grace
of Christ and accept His gift of life. Then, too, that unborn will
be accepted. To say it another way, if the mother or father accepts
Christ's gift years after the abortion, they and the unborn will have
room in the ark.

The positive, then, is that, as Christians, we should not
condemn individuals but proclaim the good news that Christ is
their Savior and is also the Savior of that aborted child. Although
we cannot condemn those who have abortions, that does not mean
we have to financially support those who make available the altar

of sacrifice. Let those who make the decision to abort pay their own way, and stop government funding to Planned Parenthood. Perhaps then we can stop the Lord our God from opening the earth and allowing it to swallow this nation.

The day after I wrote the above section, I thought of an old episode of the television program *Law & Order: SVU*, a rerun from years ago. The guest actor was Brian Dennehy, who played an older man, near death, who was seeking a meeting with his daughter. The daughter, however, refused to meet with her father because of an unforgivable lie that Dennehy's character had told years earlier. Then, once the daughter found out the reason for the lie, which was for her safety, she accepted her dad's request to see her, and the story ended with him dying after having his last words were with her. I'm trying to relate Christ's closing statement: if we forgive, God will forgive; if we cannot forgive, God will not forgive.

So, let me ask this: if an individual is killed because of an abortion by an unbelieving parent who never accepted the gift from Christ of being able to forgive, and if the sins of parents are multiplied to their children, how can it be conceivable that children will be able to forgive their parents? Americans cannot place all the blame on politicians and corporate executives. We need to be accountable for our own actions.

Chapter 13

As I read a passage of scripture this morning, I could not help replacing the word *Jerusalem* with the words *New York City*. As you read the following passage, you could replace *Jerusalem* with almost any Democratic city. (I'm rather partial to New York myself.) The following passage reflects my hope that we can still save this nation:

> Then another message came to me from the Lord Almighty. This is what the Lord Almighty says, My love for Mount Zion is passionate and strong, I am consumed with passion for Jerusalem! And now the Lord says: I am returning to Mount Zion, and I will live in Jerusalem. Then Jerusalem will be called the Faithful City ... This is what the Lord Almighty says: Once again old men and women will walk Jerusalem's streets with a cain and sit together in the city squares. And the streets of the city will be filled with boys and girls at play (Zechariah 8:1–5)

The reason this spoke so clearly to me was because the news broadcast a video of an elderly lady getting hit in the stomach and then stomped on many times for no reason. As this was happening, men stood watching from inside a restaurant, and someone closed the door. This took place in New York City, and the scripture gave me hope. What made this worse was that the person who committed this violent act was out of prison for the crime of killing his mother.

> God presides over heaven's court; he pronounces judgment on the judges: How long will you judges hand down unjust decisions? How long will you shower special favors on the wicked? (Psalms 82:1–2)

This brings me to the question of service. What exactly does it require from judges and from all the leaders in government? Emil Brunner wrote, "God does not desire 'something's from us—He desires us, ourselves: not our works, but our personality, our will, our heart" (188). The problem is that the world interprets this as slavery. In truth, they are right. The truth, however, is that when we accept the cross and the Resurrection, we find ourselves free. The freedom we feel frees us from ourselves and gives us a desire to become slaves for God. We realize we were slaves to sin, but now we are slaves to God. The difference between being a free slave and a real slave is that real slaves are held against their will. With our new freedom, there is a desire to sacrifice. Just as Christ sacrificed for us, we now have the desire to sacrifice ourselves, our personalities, our wills, and our hearts for our neighbor or our spouse or our children.

> It is his will that our service of Him should be expressed as our service to the world—through Him, and for His sake. ... [It is therefore] man's duty and privilege to live as one's whole life springs from God—the days of his anxious striving for God are over. (Brunner, 189)

What exactly does this mean? Let's consider again the issue of abortion. To express our service to the world through Him for His sake, it becomes our duty and privilege to sacrifice our lives for that of the unborn child, and this privilege springs from God. Let's consider another example. For President Biden to open the border and allow children to enter the United States, is it truly an expression of our service to the world? First of all, it was a command from God that when the Israelites entered the land promised by God, they were told not to intermarry with the inhabitants because God knew that by doing so, his children would soon lose the foundation God had established for them. As such, they would not express God's plan to the world. Second, to tell the world that our borders are now open, as Biden admitted in his first press conference, only encouraged parents in the South American countries to send their children on the long and dangerous journey north. There is no way that the God of love, the God who knows our every need, the God who has our hairs numbered, would send a child on such a journey. So how can we say this act springs from God?

How can a nation established as a forerunner, the John the Baptist of nations that is preparing for Christ's return, claim this act is a command from God? How will Biden explain before the heavenly court why he allowed thousands of children without parents to enter a nation so unjustified. (I cannot find the words to describe what I hear and see.) The real issue, as I see it, shows all the markings of a communistic and socialistic strategy to destroy our foundation of constitutional government and destroy the nation God created to give us the freedoms no other nation has, and many strive for.

To allow illegal individuals, particularly children, to enter is like allowing our five-year-old neighbor to move into our house and then to have him tell us what we must do, what we must eat, and where we can go. I don't see Biden opening his house and being dictated to by a child. I haven't heard that Nancy Pelosi has taken in a child and let him tell her where she can go.

God created humans as able to work and to create a civilization and culture with its own social life. Therefore, as former president Trump was trying to establish a policy to prohibit illegal immigration, he also sought to help the South American countries stabilize themselves with proper economic policies and input from the parents who were sending the children north.

> Only the service which God really commands is good, and this service can certainly look very different from that which man would generally imagine to be "loving service." (Brunner, 196)

Donald Trump knew that his policies looked very different, but if time had been allowed, they would have been "loving services." They were loving because they strived to keep families together and build their society safer, better economically, more secure, and free from fear. That is the kind of leadership needed in this country but also needed to help to establish freedom in other countries. The reality is that the policies established by our government for the South American countries would probably lead to many hardships for those citizens, even death. I say this because our history shows that our country, our freedoms, and our blessings came with great hardships and deaths.

There were hardships and deaths during the Revolutionary War and then in the War of 1812 (sometimes called the second war for independence). We must not forget the deaths caused by all the wars fought to retain our freedoms and blessings, including the Civil War, which unfortunately was needed to set free the slaves of our country. I occasionally watch the 1997 movie *Amistad*, which won four Academy Awards. It's a very interesting historical drama based on true events, and it stars Morgan Freeman, Anthony Hopkins,

Djimon Hounsou, and Matthew McConaughey. It's about the issue of slavery several years before the Civil War. I find it enlightening, powerful, and a reflection of the problems our nation endured.

I cannot leave this subject without facing another very real possibility—that God may be using this southern border crisis as a way to punish us. It would be one thing if our forefathers had created this nation without their profound belief, understanding of scripture, and prayers for leadership from God. But they created a nation—indeed, an entire culture and civilization—that has become known as a Judeo-Christian nation. Our friends recognize and acknowledge this truth, and our enemies recognize it as well. We, therefore, have the responsibility—and should have the privilege—to live up to our forefathers' standards, as well as the standards God has laid down for us. If we fail with these objectives, then God, as He has done in the past, will destroy us.

My fellow Americans, I started this book by telling you about the words that were spoken to me: that before I die, I will witness the destruction of this nation. Biblical history tells us there was the destruction of Judea and then Israel by the Babylonians, and the destruction of the temple and the dismantling of the Jewish government by the Romans. I have told God that I would not be disappointed if He changed his mind. But with the events of the Biden administration—and worse, the behind-closed-door meetings that have taken place—I fear my request will not be accepted. May God be with us. The aftermath of this country looks very devastating.

Chapter 14

I t's probably clear that I enjoy sharing the readings from *The Divine Imperative* by Emil Brunner. That book is over six hundred pages, and to be honest, most of what I read is confusing. I have to reread and then study it some more. Remember the rain/brain concept that reflects my ability to understand and remember things. There are, however, some things that Brunner writes that I believe reflect the human relationship with God and God's relationship with us. I believe we need to look at what Brunner calls the "calling." He begins with these words:

> God's command is wholly personal, therefore, it is wholly concrete. God never requires "something in general" … He never issues commands into the air—with the idea anyone may hear them who happens to feel like it. He tells me, or us, or you, as definite persons, to do some definite thing. (198)

This distinguishes Christians from others because the command is personal, which means that the Creator turns personally to His creation. The truth is that God does not speak only to Christians but to anyone and everyone directly. Because Luther discovered this hidden truth, which had been covered by philosophical, theological, and ethical meanderings, it had significant impact on the world. It was the rediscovery of justification by faith. Brunner says, "It meant that God wills to allow a sinful man, in all his actual sinfulness, to work for Him" (199). So, when God wills man to act here and now, it actually threatens the status quo. As such, Brunner notes,

> I can only contemplate the time behind me ... The past has been withdrawn ... is already decided. The future, however, the time which lies ahead of me, is not yet decided, and I am called to the act of decision. (200)

Are you wondering what this has to do with this nation and with our lives?

The fact that we are all sinful doesn't mean that God hasn't asked us to do specific tasks. And just because we may not have acted in the past according to our purpose, those things have passed. We are now called to decide about what we are going to do in this moment. At this point, we either withdraw from the world, or we can compromise with the world. To withdraw would be to take the easy way, but to compromise is to spend our lives in the "unceasing endeavor to alter conditions."

So, then, we have this choice. Do we, for the first time in years, follow the current events and study the candidates and vote according to the will of God—that is, for the candidates who best demonstrate their will to follow the Constitution and act for the interests of the people and not for personal gain or power? Consider those major leaders of the Democratic Party and some Republicans who seek legislation that asks for trillions of dollars for COVID relief but then only 9 percent is applied to COVID relief. Or they seek additional trillions of dollars for infrastructure work but only a small part will go to rebuilding our nation's infrastructure, as defined in the traditional definition and not with the added objectives unrelated to the physical structure of the land. The rest will be used for their personal benefits, which involves creating a socialist/communist government and tearing down our history, our culture, our Judeo-Christian society. God's commands are personal, and never have I heard him ask us to stray from the basic freedoms or to take from our neighbor.

We have made some major changes that have resulted in socialistic improvements, such as freeing the slaves and eliminating many racial laws and regulations, but people also must take responsibility for their actions, which includes seeking the truth and accepting the truth, even if it may not be to their liking. I'm thinking of such things as Antifa and Black Lives Matter (BLM) and white supremacy. BLM originally started with justifiable goals but has progressed, basically, to hatred. Their leader is a communist, and she preaches racism—hating white people and everything that they have created in this country. Their purpose now is to overthrow our society, and, along with Antifa and white supremacists, they have become angry, hateful, destructive organizations.

I recently watched a movie starring Gerard Butler titled *Machine Gun Preacher*, the story of how a roughneck American finds Jesus and is directed by God to help people in Southern Sudan. When he gets to Sudan, he finds that the people are being killed and raped; children have been kidnapped and sold as sex slaves or forced to kill as members of their captors' army. (The movie *Tears of the Sun*, starring Bruce Willis, has a similar story.) In *Machine Gun Preacher*, our hero establishes a church in his hometown and an orphanage for children in Sudan, at the same time having to fight the Lord's Resistance Army (LRA). At the end of the movie, these facts are shown on the screen:

> Amnesty International estimates that LRA as murdered 400,000 and 40,000 child abductions. They are tortured, raped, sold into sex slavery, or forced into LRA army.

What we learned from Emil Brunner is that God does use events and truths expressed in secular events to tell us His truths. Over and over throughout the history of God's first nation, which He established, He tell us of these kinds of events. They took place in nations that were not God's people, but He used those nations to do similar atrocities to His own people.

Remember that this nation was created by God for the purpose of telling the world how and why we have been blessed, but we also must realize that events, like those portrayed in *Machine Gun Preacher* and *Tears of the Sun*, can happen right here.

I'm also reminded of the movie *China Cry*, the true story of Sung Neng Yee, played by Nora Ima. After the Japanese were forced out of Shanghai by the Chinese, Sung Neng Yee became a member of the Communist Party, believing they were the liberators of her beloved Shanghai, only to find later that she had to admit that she was a Christian or deny her faith in Jesus. Although the only experience she had was her stay in a Presbyterian school during her middle-school years, it was enough for her to confess her knowledge and ultimate faith in Jesus. It was then that she was placed before a five-gun firing squad, only to have all five bullets somehow not affect her or her unborn child. You may wonder why I've mentioned these films, only because of the events that took place across our nation in the summer of 2020 by Antifa and BLM, I fear we need to confront matters of this nature. Remember that the voice I heard (and I believe it was Jesus Himself) told me that I will witness the downfall of this nation before I die. Also remember that we are out of territory—we can no longer move west—and with the downfall of God's nation, we are running out of time. That is history.

On an episode of *Fox News Sunday*, Barry C. Black, the first Seventh-day Adventist chaplain in the US Senate and former chief of navy chaplains, spoke of his prayer that had opened the Senate hearing for the second impeachment of Donald Trump. He prayed that the desired result would be achieved and then that we would have God's blessings.

I wish he would have stopped with the idea that God would achieve His desired act. Nations in the past also asked for God's blessings, and as recorded in the Old Testament, the prophets told the king not to listen to the words of assurance because God had told the nations of their upcoming destruction. I'm not praying for God's wrath but that we seek God's will. Knowing it is God's will, we then will be able to accept what happens. When God's will is done, we will find peace—maybe not the things we want, but we as individuals will have peace. As Christians, we will not become mentally ill or try to commit suicide; we will be able to accept and live. Remember that there are thousands of us, but generations will not be able to accept what will happen.

I believe we can apply to our nation the following verses from Zechariah, in which he talks about the future deliverance for Jerusalem:

> I will make Jerusalem and Judah [the United States] like an intoxicating drink to all the nearby nations … On that day I will make Jerusalem a heavy stone, a burden for the world. None of the nations who try to lift it will escape unscathed. (Zechariah 12:2–3)

We may get an intoxicating feeling when we reflect on the years that our nation was being created. We can see how other nations viewed our freedoms and our blessings of prosperity when we read books like *Democracy in America* by Alexis de Tocqueville, first published in 1835, or *A History of the American People* by Paul Johnson, first published in 1997. De Tocqueville was from France, and Johnson is from England. From the beginning of our colonies through recent times, we can say that we find strength in the Lord Almighty.

> And the clans of Judah will say to themselves, "The people of Jerusalem [America] have found strength in the Lord Almighty, their God. ... On that day the Lord will defend the people of Jerusalem [America]; the weakest among them will be as mighty as King David! (Zechariah 12:5, 8)

The weakest of them—the citizens of this country—will be as mighty as King David. These are the men and women who served in our wars to defend the gifts God has given us. These are the men and women who vote to lead our country according to the promises of the candidates.

> Then I will pour out a spirit of grace and prayer on the family of David [those who served] and on all the people of Jerusalem [the general public]. (Zechariah 12:10)

I would argue that the spirit of grace was highlighted in my parents' generation, as well as my generation, the post-World War II generation. It seems to me that during that time, many blessings were created, like the first moon landing and the many things received from that development. I believe this was the time of America's greatest achievements. Americans fought in World War II and saved the world from tyranny. The post-Vietnam generation, however, scares me.

From John, the love Gospel, we read:

> Because of the miraculous signs he did in Jerusalem at the Passover celebration, many people were

convinced that he was indeed the Messiah. But Jesus didn't trust them because he knew what people were really like. No one needed to tell him about human nature. (John 2:23–25)

I believe the Lord is telling us that Americans today recognize the wonderful things we have, and we know that millions of people from around the world have already immigrated here, but hundreds of thousands are still trying to get in. I heard that since the Biden administration opened the borders, 157 different nationalities have illegally come into the United States. They recognize the greatness of our country.

We celebrate the miraculous signs that God has shown us. Even Alexandria Ocasio-Cortez admitted that we are the richest nation in the world, yet she says we owe the world and must give away what we have. So, Jesus does not trust us because when we gather in our churches, we bow to the priests of science. When we pledge allegiance to the flag, we are now told we must omit the words "under God" because it might offend someone. God doesn't trust us because He knows what we are really like.

Emil Brunner writes in *The Divine Imperative*:

> The Calling teaches us to find the place assigned to us ... the place where we have been set in order to serve our neighbor ... First of all: we cannot tell beforehand what we ought to do; we can only learn it from our neighbor by listening to the Divine Command. And secondly: we are bidden to show love to our neighbor: but this simply means that we are to serve him. (208)

He basically says the following:

- Our neighbors are people God wills to us. He makes us aware of them.

    We are to treat them as God wants us to treat them and not as we think we need to treat them.
- We must be careful not to make our neighbors an independent entity. We must not make them more superior than what God intends because to do so would be to sever the good from what God knows are their true needs.
- We must "preserve and develop the life of our neighbor, *so far as this is possible to us*, according to our knowledge of the processes which maintain and enhance life" (Brunner, 209, emphasis mine). How, then, can we "preserve and develop" the lives of illegal immigrants if, in doing so, we destroy what God has given to us? The supreme principle, in this case, is to help the immigrants before they leave their moms and dads, their families, and their ancestral homes, before they begin their journey north. "[It] is not wrong in making happiness a subject of ethical consideration; it is only wrong in elevating it to the rank of a supreme principle" (Brunner, 209).

    I believe the following is a valid example: When the Israelites entered their promised land, God told them not to allow foreigners into their new nation and not to marry anyone outside His chosen people unless He brought them in. He directed Rehab, the prostitute who saved the Israelite spies, and she was not only saved during the destruction of Jericho, but she became a part of Jesus's heritage. On our southern border, we are elevating the actions toward our neighbors to the rank of a supreme principle. The Left is using the hardships of those in South America as an opportunity to change the foundation of our society, of our nation. Their real purpose is not to help the people coming into our nation but their own personal gain.

- We must recognize that the existing world is not the world God created. Our nation is just as sinful as the nations from which the immigrants are coming. To compel us to become what the Left and many Democrats are advocating is not necessary—their ideas of socialism and communism, leading to totalitarianism, which they try to convince us will bring stability and a utopian peace. But these historical forms have been proven to be the "imperfection of the created world":

> It is, of course, true that they are at the same time instruments of an evil, violent, collective egoism, instruments of tyranny, by means of which the collective body holds the individual in bondage, and degrades him to be the mere instrument of egoistic collective ends. (Brunner, 217)

The above words were written generations ago, yet read these words: *instruments of an evil, violent, collective egoism, instruments of tyranny.* Many argue that President Trump was trying to elevate his personal power and prestige, but he was attempting to lower the role of government and how it tries to conceal God. He repeatedly stressed the gifts of our forefathers, the freedoms as described in the Declaration of Independence, and how those rights are preserved and developed in the Constitution and the Bill of Rights.

> The modern nationalistic State is a classic example. Nothing tends more to conceal God from man than the State, for it is always able to invest itself with

a peculiar glory, almost numinous in character.
(Brunner, 617)

The greater sin, then, is for us to believe that we are superior to the South American nations and the 157 nations whose citizens have illegally come into our country since Joe Biden took office. Ocasio-Cortez wants us to accept that since we are the richest nation in the world, we are required to abolish what God has created. She and her associates seek to make us as individuals in bondage to the state, rather than having individual freedom.

After the total destruction of the temple and almost total destruction of Jerusalem in AD 70, the Sanhedrin convinced the Romans to establish a new rabbinical school in Jamnia in western Judea. It was there that the Jewish religious leaders realized that the practices they had performed in the temple could not be fully implemented in their new location.

The new Sanhedrin grasped the practical truth that "new occasions teach new duties." (Bruce, 385)

If Joe Biden's policies and the backroom secret activities continue, as they so rapidly have developed, the land that we recognize as the United States will continue to exist—people will live and continue to enjoy the land—but we will not have the Constitution or Bill of Rights. We will not have representatives as we have had throughout our history. There may be "representatives," but they'll be selected, appointed, self-serving, government masters.

Chapter 15

The southern border is a hot political issue. We must realize the potential dangers in how things are changing, and the policies being carried forward by the Biden administration. In every community, citizens are concerned with political and economic policies. The economic policies, however, affect citizens more directly and instantaneously.

I started this book with the expression of my love for this country, but I must admit that I have a subtle uneasiness and distrust with the capitalistic economic system with which we live. I've heard that the father of capitalism was John Calvin. His writings do suggest free enterprise, with individuals being the risk-takers and therefore reaping the profits. Calvin's revolutionary ideas were in reaction to the then socially accepted practices established by the Roman Catholic Church, which, in broad terms, dictated how the social economics at the time were practiced. I believe that if Calvin saw what was happening today, he would stand up in the grave and shout *no*. Even though he advocated free enterprise, he recognized the sins of gluttony and greed. The problem we have had throughout our history is the bigness of industry. The nation was basically made up of small businesses and independent farmers until the Industrial Revolution. Almost overnight, giant corporations were created, and average Americans found themselves privy to Big Brother.

Today's practices by corporate institutions have created major crises—and not for the first time. For example, we can look at the steel and railroad industries at the turn of the twentieth century. President Theodore Roosevelt regulated the companies that did interstate business because companies would alter their policies from state to state and often, they would change prices from community to community. Although presidents could not regulate individual policies, President Roosevelt advocated for and convinced Congress that the federal government could regulate corporations doing business across state lines. In effect, he protected the American citizens from unfair and unjust policies that they were unable to regulate for themselves. In the process, he united many of the corporate activities by unifying the services.

I've read that railroad companies would alter the width of their rail tracks, which prevented people from a particular area from transporting stock to another; they were forced to change railway companies, at personal cost, to complete the journey.

Today, some corporations are larger and more powerful than many countries. Major League Baseball, the Coca-Cola Company, and Delta Airlines all have made public political statements that reflect the immense power and influence corporations have on American individuals and those worldwide. I hope their results will be greatly affected by US citizens because our actions to boycott their products can determine the future sales and profits these organizations enjoy. Our choosing to purchase other products or find other forms of entertainment will tell these nation-sized organizations that we, the people, still have the power.

A more complex issue, however, are the problems that social media corporations have forced us to deal with. Like the railroads at the turn of the twentieth century, social media has no competition to which we can turn with our business. As we have seen, they have the power to control our freedoms—freedom of speech, freedom of movement without being moderated (for example, they know where we shop and what we buy), and freedom of getting complete and accurate information. Although Emil Brunner's *The Divine Imperative,* was first published in 1937, he pointed out that capitalism has major issues. Capitalism was created with an economic spirit of individual success. Individuals could create their own businesses and work to make them successful and make an honest living. Individuals also could invest their savings in other businesses and share in the profits. Socialism, particularly Marxist Socialism, however, is based on community resources. History has proven that the materials produced by the community paralyze the results of progress.

> In the economic question, anywhere at all, it is quite evident that mere technological progress, combined with the motive of profit, is unable to produce anything healthy and vital. (Brunner, 429)

That is where socialism controls the making and output of products, rather than the free market, and does not produce healthy and vital products that individuals need or desire.

It was then that ideas and new practices were brought forward by the church because it knew what a community is:

> She knows that community is not something extra added to life, but that it is the very substance of human life itself ... It is the duty of the Church— not of the Church alone, but still of the Church above all—to revive the idea of the responsibility of all for all, idea of concrete responsibility in mutual unity; for only out of this thinking and willing can a new order be created, which—while it certainly is not the Kingdom of God—does deserve to be called a "better" economic order (Brunner, 430)

I believe that if we study church attendance and individual participation, we will find that church's today have a much harder time finding individuals who are willing to give of their time to be active. It seems people think they need to be paid for their knowledge and willingness to give their time. Just as the crucifixion of Jesus Christ and the acceptance of salvation is an individual issue, so is the matter of individual survival and success.

The old saying "You can lead a horse to water, but you can't make it drink" reflects that we can offer opportunities, but we cannot make individuals accept what is available. Therefore, in the church as well as in society, there is the disturbing fact that we are losing the sense of community. The problem is that individual acts of capitalism have created a "class struggle." Although this struggle is as old as history itself, modern capitalism beginning with the Industrial Revolution has divided the two groups of people: capitalists and proletarians. The question for Christians then becomes, which of the two groups do we accept in the struggle between the classes? By fighting against the privileged, we choose the easy choice because as Christians we recognize God's concern for the poor, but is it the better order? Would it not be better to persuade the privileged to accept less and pass the profits to the poor by lowering the cost?

> [Even though an individual] is willing to go all lengths for the sake of establishing the "new order," might still feel unable to join any of these anti-capitalist groups; his [being a Christian] hesitation to do so would be due to his conviction that these groups would do more harm than good, not to themselves, but to the people as a whole. (Brunner, 431)

Today, the true dilemma of choosing how we can confront the big corporations, yet achieve a free and capitalistic society, that is a 'new order' is not clear. We have not yet discovered any real solution for how we can create a society where individual success is rewarded and the community can enjoy the benefits of what the individual has achieved, without creating class distinction and not join these "anti-capitalist groups" like the American Marxist, Antifa, and BLM. Perhaps we can learn from the results that President Trump was able to direct with the combined efforts of corporate actions uniting to find solution to the COVID-19 crisis.

For many years, I have wondered why corporate investors and CEOs have such huge personal gains. If my understanding is correct of what transpired with President Trump's leadership, I believe we may have a blueprint for future capitalism. If my understanding is correct, major-medical drug-creating companies joined in their experimental and technical investigations to create medicines and vaccines in record time. This achievement was made possible only because President Trump canceled massive amounts of government regulations, allowing for the rapid advancement of help for the American citizens. I have not yet heard of the ultimate profits these drug manufactures have accumulated from these coordinated activities, but if my understanding is correct, these companies have not taken advantage of the crisis to line their pockets with gold. If this is true, then we have an example of what might be applied to the social media issue. Also, corporate America might realize that reducing huge profits and more sharing with the community might save the nation.

These companies need to continually seek to improve their technology and services, but to allow a single organization to control the entire field of social communications is to allow that one company to establish control of freedom of speech and the ability to limit information to whatever that individual company believes is important, rather than allowing individual citizens to make their own decisions. I believe the regulations that limit the quantity of communication capacity are possible by the government without government control. Thus, breaking up the massive communications industry would allow competition and as such allow more individuals to enter into the field of communications.

The role of government is to watch for misconduct and stop it but not to dictate. The idea that it costs over a hundred dollars a month, and the owners of the media get hundred of thousands of dollars per month is not justice, and it gives many people a reason to rebel against the system. Think of the farmer in small-town Nebraska, who had to pay for rail transportation, only to have to pay again to transfer to another line at the necessary juncture, where the line from his hometown ended and goods had to be transferred to another line. Then the same procedure might have happened when the second line of rail ended, and goods had to transfer to yet a third rail line. Finally, the goods reached San Francisco or New York, but with each transfer, it was the right of each rail company to decide if the goods being transferred were satisfactory to their standards; if not, they had the right to refuse to carry the goods. It was that type of unjust practice from which President Teddy Roosevelt protected the American citizens.

Government must protect American citizens from social media. In addition, we need to protect citizens from the deliberate miscarriage of news. If news sources do not outright lie to us, they broadcast or print only parts of what someone said. They edit to meet their ideas. Many argue that free enterprise will correct this problem, but the reality is that we need protective government legislation before a free enterprise system can become available.

Malachi was pretty clear when he told the people of God:

> I am the Lord, and I do not change. This is why you
> descendants of Jacob are not already destroyed ...
> You have cheated me of the tithes and offerings due
> me. You are under a curse, for your whole nation
> has been cheating me. Bring all the tithes into the
> storehouse so there will be enough food in my
> Temple. If you do, says the Lord Almighty, "I will
> open the windows of heaven for you." (Malachi
> 3:1, 8–10)

You might be wondering how I can relate the filling of our storehouse with the above discussion. In the first illustration, President Roosevelt made it possible for innocent citizens to save a lot of money and fill their individual storerooms by forcing corporate America to unify a process. Now, our leaders must set regulations for social and commercial media to allow us the right to know the truth and keep freedom of speech so that we can intellectually analyze our candidates and monitor their actions.

There is also the reality of what I've talked about before— Alexandria Ocasio-Cortez's comment about the United States being the richest nation. As Malachi pointed out, God's request was to fill the storehouse, not to bring the people into the storehouse. In other words, God expects us to help the immigrant while they are in their native countries; then he'll open heaven. As stated earlier, to bring millions into this country will not only weaken our land but will result in their continually living in similar conditions to that which they had at home. In God's plan, He will open heaven for us, and He will take the food to them, not bring them to the food.

If you question God's promises and His ability to fulfill them, let me refer you to John 5. I'm thinking of those whose desire it is to make government the dictators of our lives. Jesus spoke of what was his witness:

If I were to testify on my own behalf, my testimony would not be valid ... In fact, you sent messengers to listen to John the Baptist, and he preached the truth. But the best testimony about me is not from man ... John shone brightly for a while, and you benefited and rejoiced. But I have a greater witness than John—my teachings and my miracles ... And the Father himself has also testifies about me ... But you do not have his message in your heart, because you do not believe me—the one he sent to you ... Your approval or disapproval means nothing to me, because I know you don't have God's love within you ... No wonder you can't believe! For you gladly honor each other, but you don't care about the honor that comes from God alone. ... But if you had believed Moses, you would have believed me because he wrote about me. And since you don't believe what he wrote, how will you believe what I say. (John 5:31–47)

Jesus does not need to testify about Himself, and He does not need to testify about what God has given to us. We have many historical events that tell us of God's creation and His gifts. Like John the Baptist, the testimony of our history—of our Declaration of Independence, our written Constitution and Bill of Rights, as well as the many articles describing the debates—shows God's work in the creation of our country and in the world. Jesus said God Himself has testified. I have already expressed many miracles that God created to save our nation and to help bless our lives. The thing is, God doesn't need our approval or our disapproval because we know what He has done in the past.

Throughout this book, I have mentioned the previous nations

that God created as representatives of Him to other nations. God did not need their approval, but He did follow their desires. As with them, God knows that if we haven't already turned our love from Him and the gifts with which He has blessed us, we are openly doing so now. If we truly believe that our history was a gift from God, then we would believe this country is the John the Baptist of nations. If we don't believe this, how can we believe what God has told us about what I believe is coming very soon?

Every generation, even the disciples, has looked for Christ's return. We must remember that a day for the Lord is like a thousand years for us. That means the crucifixion and the Resurrection were yesterday. While on the cross, Christ told the thief on the cross next to him, "Today you will be with Me in paradise." Our time is not a factor in God's kingdom. John the Baptist was killed after his brief time of glory, and so are we, as a nation, on borrowed time. As I've said many times that there is no more territory to create a new nation, and now we are destroying God's best of all worlds, so the next phase of human existence does not look good.

Remember, however, that as Christians, we must pray for God's plan to be fulfilled, and then we will be filled with the peace of God.

Conclusion

This book could go on and on—I could keep adding to it.

Every night, I watch the news, and at present, I'm reading three books: *New Testament History*, by F.F. Bruce; *Andrew Jackson and the Miracle of New Orleans*, by Brian Kilmeade and Don Yaeger; and *The Divine Imperative*, by Emil Brunner. I've also read Psalms, the Gospel of Luke, and the Gospel of John, and since I started writing this book, I've read Daniel, Hosea, Joel, Amos, Obadiah, Jonah, Micah, Nahum, Habakkuk, Zephaniah, Haggai, Zechariah, Malachi and the book of Hebrews. It seems I keep adding more to this book because the news and the reading won't let me stop—but I know I must finish.

Three days ago, my wife and I were shopping, and I found a new book—*The Book of Signs* by Dr. David Jeremiah. I purchased it because I respect Dr. Jeremiah, and the book's subject corresponds with what I've been writing. The signs I reflect on, however, and those that Dr. Jeremiah writes about may or may not be the same. If they are, it's only because God works in mysterious ways, and it is His desire that we become aware of what His signs mean.

I was going to close this book by quoting Psalms 86, but I've decided to ask you to look it up on your own. Instead, I want to quote the words of a song I have come to love; it's "He Grew the Tree/The Old Rugged Cross," as sung by the Master's Voice Quartet from Sioux Falls, South Dakota. Below are the lyrics from the song "He Grew the Tree" by Barbara Mandrell:

He molded and built a small lonely hill
That he knew would be called Calvary
He grew the tree he knew would be
Used to make the old rugged cross
With great love for man God gave with his plan
Saw him spat upon rejected and mocked
Still he grew the tree that he knew would be
Used to make the old rugged cross.

The version by the Master's Voice Quartet then leads into "The Old Rugged Cross." The difference between these words applying to God's plan for me and for you differs from God's plan that called for the suffering of His Son so that we could be free from sin. God's plan for the United States was that many suffered so that you and I could live free in the nation that I believe was created as the John the Baptist of nations. This book is intended to offer my expression of love and thanks to God, my Father, and my hope that this nation will continue long after my death.

Reference List

Bruce, F. F. *New Testament History*. Anchor Books, Doubleday & Company, Inc. Garden City, New York 1972

Brunner, Emil. *The Divine Imperative*. The Westminster Press, Philadelphia English translation by Lutterworth Press 1937

Ridderbos, Herman. *Paul: An Outline of His Theology*. Wm B. Eerdmans Publish8ing Company, Grand Rapids, Michigan 1975

Scripture References

Printed in the United States
by Baker & Taylor Publisher Services